Lynds Eugene Jones

A history of the United States for young Americans from the landing of Columbus to the inauguration of Benjamin Harrison

Lynds Eugene Jones

A history of the United States for young Americans from the landing of Columbus to the inauguration of Benjamin Harrison

ISBN/EAN: 9783337124953

Printed in Europe, USA, Canada, Australia, Japan

Cover: Foto ©ninafisch / pixelio.de

More available books at **www.hansebooks.com**

A HISTORY

OF THE

UNITED STATES

FOR YOUNG AMERICANS

*From the Landing of Columbus to the Inauguration
of Benjamin Harrison*

BY

LYNDS E. JONES

WITH 230 ILLUSTRATIONS

GEORGE ROUTLEDGE AND SONS
NEW YORK: 9 LAFAYETTE PLACE
LONDON, MANCHESTER AND GLASGOW

IN UNIFORM STYLE.

History of the United States.
History of England.

Each 160 pages, quarto. With numerous illustrations. Boards, lithographed double cover, each, 75 cents.

GEORGE ROUTLEDGE & SONS,
NEW YORK: 9 LAFAYETTE PLACE;
LONDON, MANCHESTER, AND GLASGOW.

COPYRIGHTED, 1889, BY JOSEPH L. BLAMIRE.

PREFACE.

LITTLE doubt now remains that, some five hundred years before Columbus set sail on his famous voyage, this continent was visited by the Northmen, or people from Norway and Iceland. They were a venturesome, sea-loving race, and on one of their many bold western expeditions they chanced upon Greenland and then upon the mainland. They made, however, no permanent settlement here, and the knowledge of their discovery does not appear to have travelled much beyond their own country, and seems to have been soon forgotten even there. It became a lost discovery, with little bearing upon the history of the New World and none whatever upon that of the United States. Our history—the history of the American people—only dates from the discovery, or rediscovery, of a Western Hemisphere by Columbus.

This closing year of centennial celebrations seems a peculiarly fitting occasion to attempt once more to excite in the youth of our country an interest in its past history. We are seeking in these days to do honor in every way to the Fathers of the Republic. Surely we can pay them no greater reverence than by retelling the story of their deeds as examples for our children to emulate. And if from the reading of this volume, necessarily limited to a narrative of only the most notable incidents which have marked the progress of the nation, a desire is awakened in the minds of young Americans to learn more of the land to which it is their happy fortune to belong; if a purer patriotism is aroused, and a stronger purpose formed to live a life worthy of the founders of the Union, its object will be fully accomplished.

LYNDS E. JONES.

BROOKLYN, N. Y., 1889.

CONTENTS.

CHAPTER I.   PAGE
How Columbus Found a New World, . 1

CHAPTER II.
Followers in Columbus's Track, . 5

CHAPTER III.
First Attempts to Settle North America, and their Failure, ... 9

CHAPTER IV.
The Thirteen Colonies, . . 11
   Virginia, ... 11
   New York, ... 15
   Massachusetts, . . . 18
   Connecticut, . . . 23
   Rhode Island, . . . 25
   New Hampshire, . . 26
   Maryland, ... 26
   New Jersey, . . . 27
   Pennsylvania, . . . 28
   Delaware, ... 29
   North Carolina, . . 30
   South Carolina, . . 31
   Georgia, ... 32

CHAPTER V.
The Whites and the Indians, . . 32

CHAPTER VI.
The French and Indian Wars, . . 36

CHAPTER VII.
Separation from England, . . 41

CHAPTER VIII.   PAGE
The Minute-Men at Lexington and at Bunker Hill, ... 44

CHAPTER IX.
Washington in Command, . . 49

CHAPTER X.
The Loss of Philadelphia and the Victory at Saratoga, ... 55

CHAPTER XI.
Aid from France, . . 57

CHAPTER XII.
The War in the South and Arnold's Treason, ... 59

CHAPTER XIII.
The Surrender of Cornwallis and the Close of the War, ... 61

CHAPTER XIV.
Framing the Constitution, . . 63

CHAPTER XV.
Formation of the New Government under Washington, ... 64

CHAPTER XVI.
The Beginning of Party Politics, . . 67

CHAPTER XVII.
The Administration of Jefferson, . 71

CONTENTS.

CHAPTER XVIII.
THE WAR OF 1812, ... 75

CHAPTER XIX.
THE ERA OF GOOD FEELING AND THE MISSOURI COMPROMISE, ... 81

CHAPTER XX.
THE "AMERICAN SYSTEM" AND NULLIFICATION, ... 85

CHAPTER XXI.
VAN BUREN, HARRISON, TYLER, . . 89

CHAPTER XXII.
THE MEXICAN WAR, . . . 93

CHAPTER XXIII.
THE ANTI-SLAVERY STRUGGLE, . . . 97

CHAPTER XXIV.
OUTBREAK OF THE CIVIL WAR, . . 102

CHAPTER XXV.
EVENTS OF 1862, ... 108

CHAPTER XXVI.
THE THIRD YEAR OF THE WAR, . . 114

CHAPTER XXVII.
NEARING THE END, ... 119

CHAPTER XXVIII.
THE RETURN OF PEACE, . . . 126

CHAPTER XXIX.
RECONSTRUCTION OF THE SOUTH, . 130

CHAPTER XXX.
THE PRESIDENCY OF GENERAL GRANT, . 134

CHAPTER XXXI.
MR. HAYES'S ADMINISTRATION, . 139

CHAPTER XXXII.
THE CIVIL SERVICE AND THE MORMONS, . 141

CHAPTER XXXIII.
THE MOST RECENT EVENTS, . . . 144

TABLE OF THE PRESIDENTS, . . 147
TABLE OF ADMISSION OF STATES, . . 148
CHRONOLOGICAL TABLE, . 149

CHAPTER I.

HOW COLUMBUS FOUND A NEW WORLD.

CHRISTOPHER COLUMBUS.

ica or who even knew that there was such a country. But there was one man who thought there *ought* to be such a country, and who was determined to find out for himself whether or not he was right in thinking so. Even he did not dream that America was a continent by itself. He thought that the earth was smaller than it is; that Asia extended a greater distance around it than it does; and that by sailing westward out into the ocean, further than any one had ever sailed before, he could reach India more easily than could those

ISABELLA.

THERE are two dates in the history of their country which no American boy or girl should ever forget: one is the year 1492, in which America was discovered by Columbus; the other is the year 1776, in which it freed itself from the rule of Great Britain and began to govern itself. There are many other things which they ought to know and which they will have to learn, but these are the two which above everything else they should know best of all.

Four hundred years ago there was no person living, except the Indians, who had ever been in Amer-

who had gone there by travelling towards the east.

No one believed him; every one laughed at him; for in those days few people imagined that the earth was round; they thought that it was flat; and to attempt to get to India by sailing towards the west seemed to them about as sensible as to try to reach the centre of the earth by flying away from it up in a balloon. But Columbus, for that was the man's name, did not mind their laughter. He was sure that the world was round, and that somewhere beyond the great Atlantic Ocean there must be land. And he was willing to face any possible danger in crossing this unexplored ocean to find this unknown land if some one would only fit out for him the ships which he was too poor to provide himself.

THE EMBARKATION OF COLUMBUS.

It was many years before he could get any one to do this. Those in his own country, Italy, refused; so did those in Portugal; and at first even those in Spain. At last, after ten years' constant begging, Queen Isabella of Spain helped him in obtaining three ships with which to make the attempt. These ships were all sailing vessels, for the use of steam was not at that time known. They were called the *Santa Maria*, the *Pinta* and the *Nina*, and would be thought nowadays much too small for a voyage across the Atlantic, but they were fair-sized vessels for the time, especially the *Santa Maria*, which was ninety feet long and had a deck its entire length, an advantage which the others did not share.

Columbus set sail from Spain, on what was to prove the most wonderful voyage ever made, with one hundred and twenty men and with food enough to last them all a year. The men were not very anxious to go, and some of them had to be driven on board the ships by force. Nor is it strange that they showed so little eagerness in starting on a voyage of which they could not know the end, and from which the chances seemed so great that they might never return. Like most men, the sailors cared far more for their own safety than they did for any pos-

COLUMBUS ON HIS CARAVEL.

HOW COLUMBUS FOUND A NEW WORLD.

COLUMBUS BEFORE THE COUNCIL.

men about him, who could not be trusted but who must be watched, with no one to consult or to confide in or to share anxiety with—who can imagine a loftier courage than that now shown by him in still holding fast to the same firm belief that land must lie to the westward?

For two months and more the little boats kept bravely on their way across the ocean, and then at last, on October 12, 1492, the pa-

sible glory they might win, and so their fears did not lessen as time passed on and the distance between them and their homes increased, and Columbus had to exert all his powers, coaxing and threatening by turns, to persuade them to keep on. He dared not let them know the true distance they sailed from day to day, because he knew that if they did learn this they would insist upon turning back. Once they did plan to seize and throw him overboard and then to return to Spain, but fortunately the plot was discovered and prevented.

Surely, if ever a man displayed courage, and courage of the finest and rarest kind, that man was Columbus. In spite of the jeers and laughter that greeted him he had clung steadily to his opinion that the world was round and that there was land beyond the water—and did not that take courage? During the weary years when he begged on foot from country to country for ships to find this land, did it not take courage to endure his voluntary poverty and the insults and scorn with which his requests were refused, and to suffer nothing to turn him from the path he had marked out for himself? And now, far out at sea, many weeks' journey from home, in daily danger from storm and tempest, in greater danger from the

COLUMBUS IN CHAINS.

tience and the faith of Columbus were rewarded by a sight of the land he had come so far to seek. Though it was but an island that he first saw he was content for the time, knowing that the main shore could not be far distant. With tears of thankfulness and a heart full of solemn joy he landed with his men, and, kissing the earth, claimed the island in the name of the King and Queen of Spain, whose flag he carried in his hand. Supposing that this island, which he named San Salvador (and which is one of the Bahamas), was off the coast of India, he called the natives, who had watched with the greatest astonishment the Europeans approach and land, Indians, the name which they have retained to the present time, though it was known long ago that their country was on the opposite side of the world from India.

Before returning to Spain, Columbus visited some of the West India islands but did not touch the mainland. On his second voyage from Spain, in which he had a fleet of seventeen vessels with fifteen hundred men, he discovered the Windward Islands and planted a colony on Hayti. It was not until his third voyage, in 1498, that he reached the continent, landing near the Orinoco River in South America. Finally, on his fourth and last voyage, he reached North America. He still supposed that these were the eastern shores of Asia, nor did it become known until after his death that instead of discovering a new passage to India he had discovered what was of far greater importance, a New World.

Beyond his satisfaction in proving to the world that he was right, and in adding to the world's knowledge and future wealth, Columbus gained nothing from his great discovery. On his return from his first voyage he was received with great honor. On his third voyage he returned home in chains. His best friend, Queen Isabella, was dead, and King Ferdinand, disappointed that the wealth which he expected from the New World did not flow into his treasury at once, was indifferent to him and neglected him. Even the colony which he himself had founded on Hayti, and whose governor it was that had previously sent him to Spain in chains, disowned him and would not allow him to land on the island when he stopped there on his last voyage. Worn out and broken-hearted, he died in 1506, seventy years old. After his death King Ferdinand did him tardy justice by having a monument placed over his grave on which were these words: "TO CASTILE AND LEON COLUMBUS GAVE A NEW WORLD." Two hundred years later his body was brought from Spain and placed in the cathedral at Havana, that it might rest in the New World he had discovered.

INDIAN BOATS AT THE TIME OF COLUMBUS.

CHAPTER II.

FOLLOWERS IN COLUMBUS'S TRACK.

COLUMBUS reached the mainland on his third voyage in 1498, but he was not the first to do so. When the news of his discovery became known on his return from his first voyage it aroused great interest and excitement throughout all Europe, and other expeditions were immediately sent out to make further discoveries. Among these was one under the direction of an Italian named Americus Vespucius, who visited South America in 1497, and another under command of an Englishman named John Cabot, who with his three sons landed on Labrador a little later in the same year. So that though the credit and the glory of the discovery without doubt belong to Columbus alone, others were before him in actually reaching both North and South America.

It would seem but just that if Columbus was to receive neither riches nor honors for his discovery that at least his name might have been given to the country that became known through his untiring exertions. But even this has been denied him, and the New World has been called after the man who was the first to land upon the continent, Americus Vespucius. It is only fair to add that Americus himself had nothing to do with this, but that the name was given to it by others.

Columbus, Americus and Cabot having led the way, others soon followed in their steps. Among the first to do so was a son of John Cabot, Sebastian by name, who had accompanied his father when he landed on Labrador in 1497. Sebastian made two voyages besides the one with his father, during which he explored Hudson's Bay and followed the coast from Newfoundland to Maryland. He was the first to suspect that Columbus was wrong in thinking the eastern shores of Asia had been reached; he believed, what was soon found to be the fact, that the discovery was that of a new continent. The voyages of the Cabots are especially important, as they were the chief ground for England's claim to the greater part of North America, and were the reason why

AMERICUS VESPUCIUS.

so many more colonies from England settled there than from any other country. For in those days it was the custom to add any newly discovered land to the country under whose flag the discoverer sailed. This was done whether the natives liked it or not; generally they did not like it, but that made no difference to the white men, who seemed to think that the natives had no rights to the land although they and their fathers had owned it for centuries.

Sebastian Cabot received a very different welcome on his return home from that given to Columbus. The King of England gave him a pension and every one made much of him. But this respect does not seem to have extended beyond his life, for history does not tell when or where he died, and though "he gave England a continent, no one knows his grave."

Among the wonderful stories told and believed in Europe at this time was one of a magical fountain, said to be somewhere in the New World, though no one knew just where, the waters of which, it was declared, would make forever young whoever drank of them. It was in search of this "fountain of youth" that a Spaniard named Ponce de Leon, who had been a companion of Columbus on his second voyage, set sail not long after Cabot

SEBASTIAN CABOT.

had made his discoveries. Though he did not find this "elixir of life," he did find a land blossoming with beautiful flowers, which, as the day on which he landed was Easter (1512), called in Spanish "Pascua Florida" (*feast of flowers*), he named Florida, and took possession of in the name of the King of Spain.

The zeal of the early explorers for their own country, and their desire to add to its power and extent, sometimes caused them to do very queer and absurd things. The year after Ponce de Leon discovered Florida, another Spaniard, Balboa, crossed the isthmus of Darien, and to his intense surprise found there was another ocean on the further side of it. Wading into it up to his waist, he waved his sword above his head and boldly proclaimed the King of Spain the owner and master of that vast body of water, and swore to defend his rights to it against all comers. Balboa gave to it the name of the "Sea of the South," but it was finally called the Pacific Ocean,

BALBOA DISCOVERING THE PACIFIC OCEAN.

under the mistaken belief that it was more peaceful and less stormy than the Atlantic.

Other Spaniards in the meantime explored Central and South America, the West Indies and other islands near the coast. Mexico was seized and conquered by Cortez and Peru by Pizarro, and their wealth added to the riches of the Spanish crown. The governor of the Spanish colony which had been founded on Cuba, Ferdinand de Soto, hoping to find in Florida a country as rich as Mexico, headed an expedition which landed there in search of gold in 1539. After wandering about for two years he reached the Mississippi River, but without finding the gold he sought. Disappointed at his failure he turned homewards, but died of fever on the way and was buried by his followers in the waters of the river he had discovered.

The southern part of the continent received most attention from the Spaniards, as there was to be found the gold which was their great object in coming to America. This naturally led to their settlement there and to its gradually passing under their control. Sometimes this was done by fierce wars, as in the case of Peru and Mexico, and sometimes peaceably with little or no trouble from the natives. The final result was that all of Central and South America became Spanish excepting Brazil, which fell to Portugal, the only possession of that country in the New World. But all of the discoveries and explorations in the early days of American history were not made by the Spanish and English; France did her share, and a very important share it was. As early as 1504, French fishing vessels visited the Gulf of St. Lawrence, and two years later a rough map of the

DE SOTO DISCOVERING THE MISSISSIPPI.

Gulf was prepared for the use of these fishermen by a Frenchman named Denys.

In 1524 an expedition was sent out from France under command of Verrazzano, which explored the coast from South Carolina to Nova Scotia, entering on the way the harbors both of New York and Newport. Verrazzano wrote a very full description of the Atlantic coast, the most complete of any made at that time. It is still in existence and sounds very strange now, but was remarkably accurate for that period, when so little was known about this country. Ten years after he made his voyage, another Frenchman, Cartier, came here and sailed up the St. Lawrence River (so called from Cartier's entering it on the day of that saint) a distance of fifteen hundred miles. He gave the name of Montreal to an Indian village he found on the banks of the river, and the name of New France to all of the surrounding country. On these voyages and discoveries of Verrazzano and Cartier was laid the French claim to North America, as the English one was based on those of the Cabots. For the present these claims were of slight importance and little attention was paid to them, but later on, when the

DE SOTO.

country became settled, they clashed against each other and finally led to war.

The other nations of Europe took no part in the discovery or exploration of America, except Portugal to a very small extent. No attempt was made by the early voyagers to visit the interior of the country; they devoted themselves entirely to studying the coast, opening a trade with the Indians and learning from them what they could about this New World, especially its wealth, for it was that which brought most of them here. In America they hoped to find another India, and to enrich themselves and those who sent them with the pearls and rubies, silks and shawls, spices, ivory and fragrant woods which they expected to take back to Europe. None of these were found, and at first it seemed as though the discovery would prove a barren one. Then gold was discovered in South America, and Spain eagerly seized it, and soon a rich stream was flowing into her treasury that made her the wealthiest country in the Old World. But in what is now

JACQUES CARTIER.

the United States that kind of wealth was not found in any quantity until the present century was half gone, and her other riches were not known or valued for a long period. There was not, therefore, the same inducement to hasten her settlement that there was in South America, and so it was deferred for many years.

CHAPTER III.

FIRST ATTEMPTS TO SETTLE NORTH AMERICA AND THEIR FAILURES.

CHAMPLAIN.

WHEN we read of the great age of many of the cities in the Old World it gives us a strange feeling to remember that in the United States we have but two towns that can boast of being three hundred years old, which to Rome, or Paris, or London, must seem very young indeed. And this feeling of strangeness grows stronger when we further reflect that neither of these two towns or cities was at first American or became American (that is, belonged to what is now the United States) for more than two hundred and fifty years after each was founded.

Not until Columbus and Vespucius and Cabot and all of their companions were dead, not until their discovery was over a hundred years old was any colony started in North America which managed to live. The Spanish cities of St. Augustine in Florida (1565) and Santa Fé in New Mexico (1582) are the only exceptions, and they remained Spanish until long after the Revolutionary War, and did not become part of the United States until the present century was out of its teens.

But it was not through want of trying that our country was not settled sooner, for the attempt to plant colonies was made time and time again during these hundred years, but without success. The French first tried about 1540 along the St. Lawrence River, but the climate was too severe. Then they tried (1562) in a milder region, at Port Royal in South Carolina. But here they grew homesick, quarrelled among themselves, killed their commander, and fled back to France. Two years later they again made an attempt, choosing this time as a site for their new home the St. John's River in Florida. For awhile everything went well; they got a good start and it looked as though this colony might succeed. And perhaps it would have done so had not the jealousy of the Spanish governor of St. Augustine led him to attack this French settlement and put nearly all of its inhabitants, including the women and children, to death. They were, however, soon revenged, for when the news of this butchery reached France a private soldier of fortune, named De Gourges, fitted out an expedition at his own expense, which sailed secretly to Fort Carolina (as the settlement on the St. John's River had been called), surprised the Spanish garrison in charge, and hung two hundred of them to neighboring trees.

At last, after many failures, in the early years of the new century a French colony planted itself (1605) in Acadia, the old name of Nova Scotia, and shortly after (1608) Champlain, who discovered the lake that bears his name, established another colony at Quebec. Both of these colonies thrived in spite of their wintry situation, and a start once made in this region, other Frenchmen settled themselves along the St. Lawrence and gradually took

PEREZ ON HIS WAY TO SANTA FÉ

possession of what is now the Dominion of Canada. By right of their settlement as well as of Cartier's previous discovery and exploration, this became a French province and remained so until the close of the French and Indian War (1763), when it was given to Great Britain, to whom it still belongs.

The English did not begin their attempts to colonize as early as the French, but they succeeded more quickly when they did begin. No English expedition of any kind, as far as is known, visited America for eighty years after the Cabots had been here. Then England's two great sailors, Frobisher and Drake, came—the first in 1576 and the other in 1579—but their object was to explore and not to settle. The first attempt to plant a colony was made in 1583 by Sir Humphrey Gilbert, but it failed, and on his way home Sir Humphrey lost his life. His half-brother, Sir Walter Raleigh, a favorite of Queen Elizabeth, next tried, and after first sending over vessels to explore the country and trade with the Indians, he despatched a larger party in 1585 to settle on a tract of land given him by Elizabeth, and which in her honor (as she was a Virgin Queen) he called Virginia. This party landed on Roanoke Island (now part of North Carolina) and remained there for a year, when it returned to England in a half-starved and very unhappy condition. Two years later Raleigh sent over another party, which also landed on Roanoke Island. Here the first white child was born in America. She was the granddaughter of the governor of the colony and was named after her birthplace, *Virginia* Dare. The ships which brought these colonists over after a time sailed back to England, intending to return shortly with further supplies for the settlers. But one thing and another detained them, and they did not get back to Roanoke Island for three years. When they did arrive the entire colony had disappeared and no trace of it has ever been found, so that to this day the fate of little Virginia and of her companions remains unknown. Sir Walter had now had enough of America. Though he had never been here himself, he had hoped through the colonies he had tried to start to obtain a fortune out of the land given him by the Queen. But instead of making money he had lost all he had in fitting out these unlucky expeditions, and so he was glad to sell the land in order to pay his debts. It was bought by some London merchants, who had no wish to colonize, but who proposed to open a trade with the Indians for tobacco and potatoes, two things unknown in Europe before America was discovered, but which now are to be found in almost every town or village throughout the world. Another unsuccessful English attempt to settle was made in 1602 at Buzzard's Bay, Massachusetts, by Bartholomew Gosnold, but his men would not remain and returned in the very ship that brought them over. Had that succeeded, France would not have secured the lead in colonization as she did by her Acadian settlement in 1605. As it is, both Spain and France had a foothold in America before England—but neither retained it as long.

SIR WALTER RALEIGH.

CHAPTER IV.

THE THIRTEEN COLONIES.

1. Virginia.

So much for the English failures in founding colonies. Now for their successes.

When King James came to the English throne on the death of Queen Elizabeth, he paid no attention to the title which she had given Raleigh, and which Raleigh had in turn sold to the London merchants, but he made a new disposition of the land. He divided all of North America, from Canada on the north

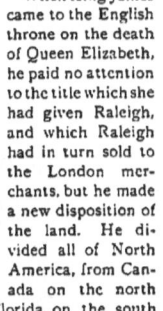

TOBACCO PLANT.

to Florida on the south (owned by the French) (owned by the Spanish), into two parts, and gave the northern half to the Plymouth Company and the southern half to the London Company. And to prevent any quarrelling between the two, the King forbade either to make any settlement within one hundred miles of the other.

These companies consisted each of a number of Englishmen who had the means to send out parties better prepared in every way to overcome the difficulties which had been too much for those who had tried before. Mexico and South America were yielding a great deal of gold at this time to Spain, and these companies were formed in the hope of obtaining gold also from North America by means of the colonies they intended to plant here.

Both companies despatched colonists about the same time; the Plymouth Company to Maine and the London Company to Virginia. The former did not prosper and were soon forced to abandon their settlement near the mouth of the Kennebec River, but the latter were more fortunate. Intending to land where Raleigh's men had landed, on Roanoke Island, they were driven out of their course by a storm into Chesapeake Bay, where they discovered a river, which they ascended for fifty miles, and there, in May, 1607, they made a settlement, which they loyally called Jamestown, in honor of their King, whose name they also gave to the James River. This was the beginning of the State of Virginia and of the United States of America.

At the start they had a hard struggle to live. The settlers were not of the stuff that colonists should be made of. There were no farmers, carpenters, or other mechanics among them; but they were mostly bankrupt gentlemen, who had come to America, as had so many others before them, in search of gold with which to repair their ruined fortunes. They neither knew how to labor with their

THE BUILDING OF JAMESTOWN.

hands nor were willing to do so had they known how, and were utterly unfitted for the rough work which always has to be done in a new country.

But they had other troubles in addition to those caused by their own ignorance and incapacity.

QUEEN ELIZABETH.

They had arrived too late in the season to plant crops for that year and had used up most of their food on the voyage, so that hunger soon stared them in the face. Many of them became sick, and all suffered greatly from the cold during their first winter, as the miserable huts they built could not give them sufficient shelter. Disappointed at not finding gold, and disheartened by the many privations they had to endure, they would quickly have deserted their newly-made home and returned to England, had it not been for one man, Captain John Smith, who kept up their courage, obtained food for them from the Indians, induced them to work, showed them how to build log-houses, settled their quarrels, and in general managed their affairs for them until they picked up heart by the arrival of further supplies of men and provisions from England.

John Smith is one of the most striking men in early American history. He had led a roving life and met with a great many strange adventures, if we are to believe the stories he tells of himself. He explored the country about Jamestown, and usually was on good terms with the Indians, though once he narrowly escaped losing his life at their hands. Powhatan, a chief not friendly to the whites, captured him and condemned him to death, and the sentence was about to be carried out when Powhatan's young daughter, Pocahontas, threw herself in front of Smith and begged his life from her father. She afterwards married a white man named Rolfe, and went to England, where she died.

In time the affairs of the little settlement began to brighten. A more industrious class of emigrants joined it, and, giving up the useless search for gold, the colonists turned their attention to raising tobacco, which they sent to England in exchange for clothing and whatever else was needed. Tobacco soon became the principal product of the colony and was used as money in buying and selling, and we read that when, later on, a number of young women were sent over for the planters to marry, their husbands paid a hundred pounds of tobacco apiece for them, some indeed as much as a hundred and fifty pounds.

By the end of the first ten years, the colony had become strong enough to take care of itself, and soon after obtained from the King and the Com-

THE THIRTEEN COLONIES. 13

pany the right to make its own laws. Accordingly, in 1619, the first legislature, or House of Burgesses as it was called, ever elected in America met at Jamestown. It is a curious fact that in the very year the colonists began to govern themselves they began to enslave others; for it was in 1619 that the first negroes were brought to Virginia by a Dutch trading vessel and sold there as slaves.

The London Company retained control of Virginia until 1624, when the King took away its charter, and she became what was known as a royal colony, or colony whose governor was appointed by the crown. He did not, however, alter the constitution previously given her, and generally the colonists were allowed to manage their own affairs. They sided with the Stuarts during the Civil War in England, and when Charles II. regained his throne Virginia proudly called herself his "ancient dominion," and this gave her the name of "The Old Dominion," which she still bears. But Charles showed no more gratitude to the Virginians for their loyalty to him and to his father than he showed to English cavaliers. He gave his assent to the oppressive navigation laws, which forbade the colonists from trading with any one but the English or from using any but English vessels to trade in, and twice he made a present of the colony to court favorites —though each time he afterwards recalled the gift.

Virginia grew very rapidly, after her early troubles were over, through emigration from England, and was the most populous as well as the oldest of the colonies. The fertility of the soil, which enabled her to raise large crops of tobacco at but little expense, made her the richest and most prosperous colony as well. Her territory was then far larger that it is now. In fact, at first it included pretty much all of our present Southern States as far south as South Carolina, and extended westward indefinitely. New colonies and (after the Revolution) new States were carved out of it, and so its area was gradually reduced to its present size.

CAPTAIN JOHN SMITH.

POCAHONTAS.

There were but few cities or towns, the people living chiefly on large plantations some distance apart. This caused the population to be so scattered that schools were not as common as in the New England colonies, and less attention was paid to education. The wealthy planters sent their sons to England to be educated and had their daughters taught in their homes. But the children of the less wealthy for the most part remained unschooled. Eighty-five years passed after the settlement at Jamestown before the first college was founded— that of William and Mary, established at Williamsburgh in 1692—though Massachusetts had had one then for more than fifty years.

Most of the settlers in Virginia were members of the Church of England, and that was therefore made the religion of the colony. Though laws were passed excluding those who held a different belief, there was no active religious persecution, and in that respect Virginia appears in a more favorable light than many of the other colonies, which not only excluded those whose faith did not agree with the prevailing one of the community, but which imprisoned and punished them if found within the colonial territory.

The relations of the Virginians with the Indians were most of the time pleasant and friendly, but there were occasional difficulties. The first occurred in 1622, and was caused by Indian jealousy at the growing size and number of the plantations, which were slowly driving the Indians back from

CAPTAIN SMITH TAKEN PRISONER BY THE INDIANS.
(*From Smith's Virginia.*)

the settlements. Three hundred and fifty whites lost their lives in this war, which was not ended until after a long and bloody contest. A second outbreak followed twenty years later, during which five hundred settlers were killed, but in which the Indians were so thoroughly beaten that they did not rise against the whites again. But the Maryland Indians sometimes made raids over the borders of Virginia, and this led in 1676 to trouble among the colonists themselves. Sir William Berkeley

POCAHONTAS SAVING CAPTAIN SMITH'S LIFE.

was at the time Governor of Virginia, and was a very unpopular one. He refused either to put down the Indians himself or to supply the settlers with arms to do so for themselves. A young planter, named Bacon, thereupon raised a body of troops, overcame the Indians, and then marched against the governor and drove him out of Jamestown, which during the struggle was burnt and has never been rebuilt. The sudden death of Bacon ended the rebellion, but Berkeley in revenge hung twenty-two of Bacon's followers, a measure so cruel that it caused good-natured King Charles to say, "The old fool has hanged more men in that naked country than I did in all England for the murder of my father."

2. New York.

One of his own courtiers remarked of James I., that "he never said a foolish thing and never did a wise one," and certainly his forbidding the London and Plymouth Companies from making any settlement within one hundred miles of the other showed as little wisdom as any act of his reign. For instead of preventing quarrels between colonies, as he intended, it caused quarrels. And it caused them in this way. By placing the English settlements so far apart, ample room was left for some other nation to slip in and plant colonies between them, and colonies of different nations near together are much more apt to quarrel than when both speak the same language and come from the same country.

And that was exactly what did happen. The Dutch seized this unoccupied land, settled it, and soon began to quarrel with the English and other colonists who established themselves in the neighborhood not long after the Dutch.

In 1609 an association of merchants in Holland, engaged in trade with the Indies, sent Hendrik Hudson to discover if there was not some passage *through* America which would shorten the distance to India—the great desire of all European traders at that time, and indeed at the present time. While trying to find such a passage he entered the Hudson River (named after him), and sailed up it to what is now the City of Hudson, which was as far as his little vessel, the "Half-Moon," could go; though one of his boats ascended it still further, to the site of the present City of Albany. When he found that he could not reach India by that route he returned to Holland.

The "Half-Moon" was the first European ship to visit the waters of the great river, and, in virtue of that fact, Holland claimed all the territory lying on both sides of it, and gave the name of the New Netherlands to the whole region. Hudson reported the natives as friendly and willing to trade with the whites, and Dutch merchants at once sent out vessels to open a traffic with the Indians. Trading-posts were soon established at various points on the river to help this traffic, which was a very profitable one to the Hollanders. An accident to one of the vessels detained its crew on Manhattan Island in 1614, and this was the beginning of the settlement of the city, which the Dutch called New Amsterdam, but which is now known to all the world as New York. Ten years later the entire island was bought from the Indians for the sum of twenty-four pounds sterling, or one hundred and twenty dollars in our money.

JAMES I.

HENDRIK HUDSON.

New Amsterdam and the New Netherlands at first grew slowly, only poorer emigrants coming over from Holland. But after a little this changed. The Dutch West India Company secured control of all of the New Netherlands from the government of Holland, and it induced a wealthier class to come and settle along the Hudson by granting to each a tract of land, sixteen miles along the banks of any stream and extending back from the stream as far as each colonist chose. They could not take land already occupied, and they were obliged to pay the Indians for what they took, as the Dutch wisely wished to preserve the friendship of the Indians. These proprietors were called "Patroons," and their tracts after Hudson's voyage. To mark these claims as well as to aid the fur-traders, forts were built, one at Hartford and one near Camden. The English disputed the claim to Connecticut (the settlement of which they had by this time begun) as indeed they had previously done the claim to the New Netherlands, and there was almost constant trouble between the two colonies, which was not ended until the present boundary line was agreed upon in 1650. On the southern side of the New Netherlands, difficulties also arose with some Swedes who had settled near Wilmington, Delaware, and which resulted in their complete conquest (1655) by the Dutch under Peter Stuyvesant, the last and the best of the four

THE "HALF MOON" AT THE MOUTH OF THE HUDSON.

"Manors." Each had the right to found a colony of fifty persons and had absolute power over his own manor, without regard to the colonial government. To aid them in tilling their land, the Company agreed to supply them with negro slaves from Africa.

For the protection of those engaged in trading with the Indians, several forts were erected, one of which (Fort Orange) was the origin of the capital city of the State, Albany. The Dutch claim included not only the present limits of New York, but also territory north and south of it, extending from Cape Cod to Cape Henlopen. This claim had for its basis explorations made by Dutch seamen soon

governors (or directors) who ruled over the New Netherlands until it passed into the possession of the English. By their just and wise treatment of the natives, the Dutch for the most part escaped the Indian wars, which were such a scourge to many of the other colonies. Only one serious disturbance occurred (1643), and that was brought on by the cruelty of the Dutch governor, Sir William Kieft, who in consequence was recalled by the West India Company, and was succeeded by Stuyvesant, who quickly made peace with the Indians.

As the colony grew in numbers and in wealth, many English joined the Dutch in New Amsterdam to share in the rich trade which had been established between the Indians on the one side and Europe on the other. This trade was largely in furs, though they also exported other articles, as tobacco and tar. Furs were sometimes used as money, much in the same way that tobacco was used in Virginia, and we hear of a minister receiving one hundred and fifty beaver-skins for his year's salary. Besides the English, many other nations had representatives there, and it was said that one could hear eighteen different languages spoken in the streets of New Amsterdam while it was still a Dutch town.

But next to the Dutch, the number of Englishmen much to the disgust of old Peter Stuyvesant, who thought them great cowards for not preferring to fight. This was in 1664, when Charles II. was on the English throne. He made a present of the colony to his brother James, the Duke of York, and the names both of the New Netherlands and of New Amsterdam were changed, in honor of the royal owner, to New York.

Holland made one attempt to regain her lost colony (1673) and for a brief time succeeded, but was forced the next year to give it back again to England.

PETER STUYVESANT.

was the largest in the place, and they in time became very much discontented with the Dutch government. It was too strict to please them. They wanted greater freedom and a voice in the management of public affairs. Many of the Dutch citizens sympathized with them in this feeling, for they, too, felt that they had much less liberty than the people in the other colonies enjoyed. When, therefore, an English fleet appeared before New Amsterdam and demanded its surrender, all of the inhabitants, the Dutch as well as the English, insisted upon giving it up,

Its new owner, the Duke of York, was more liberal than the West India Company had been. He allowed the colonists to make their own laws and granted them a charter. This he afterwards tried to recall when he became King, but he did not succeed. The number of English settlers soon exceeded the Dutch, and Dutch customs gradually disappeared, though a few have remained to the present day; for both Santa Claus and New Year's calls have come down to us from the Knickerbockers. Many years passed before the Dutch language entirely ceased to be spoken, and schools could be found in New York for a long time where English was taught like a foreign language, only as an accomplishment.

The history of New York from its conquest to the Revolution, is chiefly the history of a succession of bad governors sent by the English kings to rule over the colony, and in this its experience was the same as that of many of the other colonies. Though some of these rulers were worse than others, none of them were good or fit to govern. The colony, while large in territory, was small in population, with few settlements excepting those scattered along the Hudson River, and it remained among the less important colonies until after the independence of the country had been for some time secured.

The introduction of slavery into Virginia was followed by its introduction into all of the colonies, though it was never as extensive in the North as in the South. In New York it was the cause of a most remarkable excitement in 1740, when there was a rumor that the negroes had made a plot to kill all the whites, and before the furore could subside thirty-two negroes had been put to death and seventy-one banished. It is no longer believed, now, that such a plot had been formed, or that the slaves had in any way conspired against their masters.

3. Massachusetts.

About the time that the little colony at Jamestown was making its start, a body of men had gone to Holland from England to escape the persecutions which religious differences had brought upon them in Great Britain. In Holland they found men who believed as they did, and with whom they could

NEW AMSTERDAM IN 1659.

A, the fort; B, the church; C, the windmill; D, the flag which is hoisted when vessels arrive in port; E, the prison; F, the house of the general; G, the place of execution; H, the place of expose, or pillory.

therefore live in peace. But after spending twelve years in Holland, they became desirous of having a home of their own, where their children could grow up in English and not in Dutch ways, and which would also serve as an asylum for others, who, like themselves, might wish to leave England for "conscience' sake." So they turned their eyes to the New World, hoping there they might find a country large enough for all, and where they could worship God in the only way that seemed to them right.

Obtaining from the London Company permission to settle in "Southern Virginia," as the half of the country given that Company by King James was called, a part of their number returned from Holland to England, and being joined by others from London, set sail from Southampton in September, 1620, in the "Mayflower." They had already received the name of Pilgrims when they first went to Holland, and now the name was applied to them more seriously than ever, when they started on that greater and much more dangerous journey to America.

TOMB OF THE MATE OF THE "MAYFLOWER."

After a weary voyage of sixty-three days they reached Cape Cod, and though this was north of the limits of "Southern Virginia," they were so worn out by their confinement on the ship that they decided to make their settlement there, and accordingly on the 21st of December, 1620, they landed at a spot which they named New Plymouth, and the colonization of New England was begun.

One hundred and one sailed from Southampton on the "Mayflower." One hundred and two landed at New Plymouth; for on the voyage a little girl had been born, Peregrine White, who received her name on account of the "peregrinations" (or wanderings) of her parents. Her fate was not as sad as was that of Virginia Dare, for fortunately the Plymouth Colony did not disappear like the one on Roanoke Island, but survived its many hardships, and forms to-day a part of the great State of Massachusetts.

MONUMENT COMMEMORATING THE LANDING OF THE PILGRIMS AT PLYMOUTH.

It was a dreary and bleak shore on which they landed that cold winter day; but they had stout hearts ready to face every trial for the sake of a home for themselves and for their children. Unlike the Virginia settlers, it was not gold or the desire for riches that had tempted them to cross the Atlantic, but a love of freedom and a religious impulse, and this gave them greater courage to endure the sufferings before them. Apart from the motive which brought them to America, they were better

20   HISTORY OF THE UNITED STATES.

fitted in other ways for the task before them than were the earliest Virginians. They had stronger bodies, they were more used to hard work and were less afraid of it, and they better understood in advance what colonization really meant. And so, though the climate was more severe and the soil less fertile at Plymouth than at Jamestown, there was more cheerfulness and less discontent in this northern colony than there had been in the southern one.

Before leaving the "Mayflower," the Pilgrims chose from among their number John Carver as their governor and agreed upon a form of government which gave each one an equal voice in the management of the affairs of the colony. This was necessary because they had no charter from the King, and because their settlement was beyond the limits of the land granted to the London Company (which had sent them to this country), and therefore outside of its authority. They also organized a body of soldiers for protection against the Indians, should it be necessary, and appointed Miles Standish its captain.

The first thing done on landing was to erect a building large enough to give them all shelter in the cold weather. Then they divided themselves into nineteen families, and gradually a house was built for each. The houses were not very large, and the beds had to be pretty close together, but the colonists were much more comfortable in them than they had been on shipboard, or when they were all crowded together in the building they first occupied. They were made of logs and mortar with thatched roofs, and the windows had oiled paper in place of glass. A shed was also put up to cover their goods, and a small hospital and a church were built. As it was winter, of course no crops

PILGRIMS ON THEIR WAY TO CHURCH.

could be raised, so they supported themselves by hunting and fishing until the season came round when they could grow corn. Fortunately the Indians in their neighborhood were friendly, and a treaty was made with Massasoit, their chief, which lasted over fifty years. Though that first winter was a hard one and half of their number (including Governor Carver) died before it was over, the Pilgrims did not lose heart, and not one of them returned in the "Mayflower" when she sailed back to England the following spring. All preferred to remain and share the fate of the rest.

THE THIRTEEN COLONIES.

A few years after the landing of the Pilgrims, another body of Englishmen came over and established themselves (1628) at a point on the coast north of Plymouth, which they named Salem. Others followed them in the next year and settled at Charlestown, and soon after Boston, Roxbury and other places near by began their existence. These were all under one government and formed the Massachusetts Bay Colony. Its leading spirits were John Winthrop, John Endicott, Sir Henry Vane and John Cotton, who had obtained a charter from King James before they left England, and a grant of land from the Council of Plymouth (which had succeeded to the rights of the Plymouth Company), extending from three miles south of the Charles River to three miles north of the Merrimack River.

Members of the Massachusetts Bay Colony were known as Puritans, and, like the Pilgrims, had left England to escape religious persecution. They differed from the Pilgrims on some points of belief, but in the main were men of very much the same character—hardy, self-denying and austere. They had greater wealth and they came over in larger numbers, but their sufferings and privations during their first years in America were nearly as severe as were those of the Plymouth settlers, notwithstanding the greater comforts they had been able to provide themselves with. The two colonies maintained a separate existence for many years after their foundation, but their history and interests were the same, though the Bay Colony received by far the greater number of recruits from England, and was always larger, stronger, and more prosperous than Plymouth Colony. In 1691 the two were united under the name of Massachusetts Colony; so called from a tribe of Indians that lived close at hand—the word "Massachusetts" meaning "blue hills."

Pilgrims and Puritans both fled to this country to obtain religious freedom, but it was freedom for themselves and not for others that they sought. We have seen in Virginia that the very year the colonists began to govern themselves they began to enslave others. So in Massachusetts, as soon as the colonists escaped being persecuted themselves, they began to persecute others. In 1635 a minister in Salem, named Roger Williams, was banished from the colony because his opinions on religious matters were not quite the same as those of the others; and two years later a woman (Mrs. Hutchinson) was also driven into the wilderness for holding meetings of her own sex, in which some new views of theology were advocated. Many others fared as badly and were forced to seek a home where best they could beyond the limits of Massachusetts.

Fortunately one was soon ready for them in Rhode Island, founded by Roger Williams when he was expelled by the Puritans.

The Quakers (or Friends) were treated still more harshly. Four of them were hanged and a number of others were thrown into prison for neglecting to obey the order to leave the colony and to keep away from it. Such extreme measures and the patience and courage with which they were borne soon, however, produced a reaction in public opinion, which caused the persecution to cease and allowed the Quakers to remain undisturbed.

The history of Massachusetts was stained with yet one more persecution before religious toleration gained the day. At that time it was a common belief all over the world that there were witches

JOHN ENDICOTT.

who had the power to harm man or animal, and who could assume whatever shape they chose. In 1692 a craze broke out in Salem that there were witches there and, before people recovered their senses, twenty persons had been put to death who were innocent of any offence.

But if there was less religious freedom in Massachusetts in its earlier days than there was at the same period in Virginia, there was a greater interest in education. In all of the New England settlements, as soon as the houses and churches were built, schools were started and, before the Massachusetts Bay Colony was ten years old, Harvard College was founded at what was then Newtown, but is now Cambridge. It received its name from John Harvard, who gave to it his library of books and

HISTORY OF THE UNITED STATES.

WITCHCRAFT AT SALEM VILLAGE.

England, and for three years Massachusetts suffered under his tyranny (1686-1689), until the English Revolution gave the colonists an opportunity to rid themselves of Andros by sending him back to Great Britain. When the two colonies of Plymouth and Massachusetts Bay were united by William and Mary in 1691, a new charter was granted in place of the one recalled by James. This did not restore to the people the privilege of choosing their own governor; that was reserved for the sovereign. But it did give religious free-

about four thousand dollars in money. Harvard University (as it is now named) is thus not only the largest and richest college in America but is also the oldest.

Both in Plymouth Colony and in Massachusetts Bay Colony the governors were elected by the people (church-members only voting in the latter) until James II. ascended the English throne. He took away this right and declared that all charters previously granted to the colonies were forfeited. Sir Edmund Andros was appointed by him governor of the whole of New

HARVARD COLLEGE, CAMBRIDGE.

dom to all excepting Roman Catholics, and it extended the limits of the colony so as to include Maine and Nova Scotia. The former remained part of Massachusetts from this time until its admission as a separate State into the Union, in 1820. The latter was lost during the Revolutionary War.

4. Connecticut.

Connecticut, like Massachusetts, had at first two separate colonies within its borders, the government of each being entirely distinct from the other. There was indeed also a third settlement, but as that was small and was soon united with one of the others, it scarcely need be spoken of as an independent colony.

The first of the three was settled by colonists from Massachusetts who, in 1635 and 1636, forced their way through the wilderness and established themselves at Windsor, Hartford and Wethersfield, taking the name of the Colony of Connecticut, which in the Indian tongue means "long river." Trouble soon arose between them and the Dutch in the New Netherlands, who had previously (1633) built a fort just below Hartford, and who claimed a right to all of the land as far as Cape Cod, through explorations made by their trading vessels about the time New Amsterdam was founded. Though it caused ill-feeling and was a serious annoyance to each side, this trouble fortunately did not lead to any actual war, and it was finally settled (1650) by a treaty which placed the boundaries very much as they exist between the two States to-day.

These Connecticut colonists from Massachusetts who were so emphatic in their denial of the Dutch claim to the land they had taken possession of, had really no right to it themselves, as they had obtained no grant from the Council of Plymouth. In fact the Council of Plymouth no longer owned it, as it had previously disposed of it to the Earl of Warwick, who in turn had transferred it to Lords Say and Brook. The latter, however, made little use of it, only one small settlement being started by them, which, from their two names, was called Saybrook. It was at the mouth of the Connecticut River, and at first was only a fort, built to prevent the Dutch from gaining control of the river. It was the least important of the three independent settlements already referred to, and afterwards (1644) became part of the Colony of Connecticut.

Saybrook, Windsor and Hartford were founded about the same time, and New Haven was not long in following, but, unlike the others, it was settled (1638) by colonists who came to it directly from England and not from Massachusetts. They bought their land from the Indians and adopted the Bible as the only law of the colony, limiting the rights to vote for governor and other officers, as Massachusetts Bay had done, to church members (Puritans). This was in contrast to the Colony of Connecticut, which gave the privilege of voting to all residents of good character. As a consequence of this greater liberality, the latter colony grew more rapidly than New Haven, as new settlers who were not Puritans preferred to be under a government in which they had a voice in the management of affairs.

Neither colony obtained a charter until after the Restoration in England, when Gov. Winthrop, of the Colony of Connecticut, obtained one from Charles II. (1662), covering the territory of both and providing for their union. New Haven was not very willing to give up her independence, but finally consented, and in 1665 the two colonies became one

under the name of Connecticut. The charter was a liberal one, allowing the people to make their own laws as well as to choose their own governor and to elect their own assembly, and it was so well liked by the people that they kept it in force for more than forty years after the Declaration of Independence was adopted. James II. attempted to revoke it, as he revoked those of Massachusetts and the other colonies when he tried to unite all New England into one province with Sir Edmund Andros as its governor. Andros went to Hartford in 1687 and demanded that tree became known as the Charter Oak, and was justly the pride of Hartford, until it was blown down by a storm in 1856.

When the two colonies were united, New Haven (city) and Hartford were both made capitals of Connecticut, the governor living part of the time in one place and part of the time in the other, and this was continued after the Colony became a State; but since 1873 Hartford has been the only capital.

In 1701 Yale College was founded by the Assembly of Connecticut, at Saybrook, as a school for

THE CAPITOL, HARTFORD.

the charter be given up to him. The people objected. He insisted; a discussion followed, during which the lights (it was in the evening) were suddenly put out and in the confusion and darkness the charter mysteriously disappeared and could not be found when the lights were restored, so that Andros was compelled to go back without it. When James left the throne and the colonists felt safe once more under William and Mary the charter was brought from its hiding-place, a hollow oak tree, near at hand, where it had lain concealed for two years. This training young men to the ministry, and a few years later (1717) it was removed to New Haven, when it took its present name from Elihu Yale, the governor of the colony and a warm friend of the college. Yale was thus the third of the higher institutions of learning to be established in the country, and is next to the oldest of those still in existence, its only senior being Harvard. Next in age came the College of New Jersey (1746), the University of Pennsylvania (1749), and Columbia, formerly King's College (New York City, 1754).

5. Rhode Island.

It was in the depth of winter when Roger Williams, banished from his church in Salem, left the Colony of Massachusetts to find a home where there should be perfect religious freedom for all, whatever their belief might be. Ignorant of the way and without a guide, he wandered in the pathless woods for fourteen weeks before he found a shelter or a refuge, and when he did find it, it was among a tribe of Indians called the Narragansetts. They were very kind to him and gave him a tract of land, which, in remembrance of "God's merciful providence to him in his distress," he named Providence (1636). Others joined him there, and in the following year a settlement was also made on the Island of Rhodes, which was bought from the Indians for the purpose, and the name of which was afterwards changed to Rhode Island (or "red island," from the Dutch). Though these two colonies were entirely separate from each other, each having its own government, they served alike as a home for all who had been persecuted elsewhere, and it was said that any one who had lost his religion would find it in Rhode Island.

In 1644 a charter was obtained from the English Parliament uniting the two colonies under the name of "Rhode Island and Providence Plantations," which is still their legal name to-day. Newport (at the southern end of the Island of Rhodes) and Providence were both made capitals of the colony and are now of the State. On the accession of Charles II. a new charter was granted, confirming the colonists in all their liberties and giving them

ample powers of self-government. This charter was suspended while Andros was governor of New England (1686–1689), but afterwards resumed its force and continued to be the basis of law until 1842.

There is little of interest or importance in the early history of Rhode Island. The Indians gave her scarcely any trouble, and her principal difficulties were with Massachusetts, who, on account of her religious toleration, tried to prevent all trading and other communications between the two colonies. When Roger Williams went to England to obtain a charter Massachusetts would not allow him to sail from Boston, so that he was obliged to start from New Amsterdam. She also had disputes about her boundaries with both Massachusetts and Connecticut, who between them claimed pretty much all her territory, excepting the islands in Narragansett Bay, but she was firm and insisted upon her rights, and the matter was as last settled in 1741,

PROVIDENCE, RHODE ISLAND.

giving her the land she claimed and which she now occupies.

None of the other colonies had laws as gentle or liberal as Rhode Island or granted as much freedom to their inhabitants. Indeed they were so afraid of tyranny that when Williams refused to be their governor, they went without one for forty years to avoid the danger of choosing one who might prove a tyrant.

it grew very slowly and from its exposed position suffered a great deal from Indian attacks, its inhabitants seemed to thrive, and at the outbreak of the Revolution it was a strong and resolute colony. During much of its early history the settlers were engaged in disputes with Mason's heirs, who, though they had a legal right to the land, found it impossible to gain possession of it and were at length compelled to give up their attempts to drive the settlers

WILLIAMS' PRAYER-MEETING HOUSE, PROVIDENCE.

6. *New Hampshire.*

Religion had nothing to do with the settlement of New Hampshire, as it had with the other New England colonies. Fishing was the attraction which led to the starting in 1623 of little villages at Dover and Portsmouth, which for fifty or sixty years remained very small, being scarcely anything more than mere fishing stations. It received its name from the English county (Hampshire) in which lived John Mason, to whom the Council of Plymouth had granted the land in 1622.

Its history is closely connected with that of Massachusetts, to which it was three times formally united and from which it was as many times separated. It was also once made part of New York. Though

off and were forced to allow them to remain on it in peace.

7. *Maryland.*

As Massachusetts was settled by persecuted Pilgrims and Puritans, so Maryland was settled by persecuted Roman Catholics, whose sufferings for their religion in England were even greater than those of the Pilgrims and Puritans.

At first they attempted to found a colony in Newfoundland, but climate and soil were both against them and the attempt had to be abandoned. Next they planned to join the settlement in Virginia, but the sentiment there was too strongly opposed to Roman Catholics to permit of it. So a tract of land north of the Potomac was obtained for them from Charles I. and in honor of his wife (Henrietta Maria) was named Maryland.

This land was actually given to Lord Baltimore (Sir George Calvert), a prominent Catholic and formerly a member of the London Company. He had greatly interested himself in finding a home for his fellow-Catholics in America, had started the Newfoundland colony and had endeavored to obtain their admittance to Virginia. Before the patent (or title-deed) was signed by the King, Calvert died, and the name of his son, Cecil Calvert, who by his father's death had become Lord Baltimore, was thereupon inserted in the deed in place of his father's. This patent gave Maryland to Lord Baltimore and to his descendents forever, and they did remain its proprietors until the Revolution.

The first settlement in Maryland was made near the mouth of the Potomac in 1634, and was called St. Mary's. Annapolis, now the capital of the State and the place where the United States Naval Academy is situated, was founded in 1683, and Baltimore in 1729. Virginia was very jealous of the new colony and made her all the trouble she could. The tract given Calvert had been part of her own territory and had been taken away by Charles without her consent or knowledge just as she was about colonizing it. But though her opposition created difficulties and even caused some bloodshed, Lord Baltimore retained his rights and the colony prospered.

Though founded for and by Roman Catholics, Maryland gladly welcomed all Christians by whatever name they called themselves to her settlements. In this respect she was more liberal than any of the other early colonies, excepting only Rhode Island, who did not limit her welcome to Christians, but who received Jew and sceptic as freely as Baptist or Churchman. Maryland was equally liberal in political matters, giving every settler an equal vote in making laws for the colony.

This liberality the Catholics afterwards had reason to regret, for it caused so many Protestants who had been persecuted elsewhere to take refuge in Maryland that in time they outnumbered the Catholics and then ungratefully deprived the latter of the right to vote in the very colony founded especially for them.

Maryland had no trouble with the Indians, and, excepting the early difficulties with Virginia, lived at peace with all the world. When Pennsylvania was colonized a difference of opinion arose between her and Maryland regarding the boundary line between the two colonies, which was not settled till the year in which the French and Indian war was ended (1763). The division line then agreed upon was called, from the names of the two surveyors who ran it, "Mason and Dixon's line," and served

HENRIETTA.

not only to separate Pennsylvania and Maryland but for a hundred years marked in popular speech the boundary between the free and the slave States.

8. New Jersey.

New Jersey had been part of the New Netherlands, and, on the surrender of the latter to the English in 1664, passed with the other possessions of the Dutch into the ownership of the Duke of York, who sold it the same year to Lord Berkeley and Sir George Carteret. The latter gave it its name from the Island of Jersey, in the English Channel, of which he had once been governor.

Though the Swedes and Dutch had begun some small settlements there soon after New Amsterdam was founded, they were of little account, and the real colonization of New Jersey may be said to have started with Elizabeth, settled in 1664 by Puritans from Long Island. Connecticut emigrants settled Newark in 1666, and the Quakers Burlington in 1677. In 1676 Berkeley and Carteret divided the tract between them, East Jersey falling to the latter and West Jersey to the former. Gradually the Quakers bought up most of the land, and with some Scottish Presbyterians became the principal settlers. There was perfect liberty of conscience throughout the colony, which in this respect resembled Rhode Island and Maryland. It passed out of the possession of the proprietors in 1702 and became a royal colony. For a time it was made part of New York, though with a separate assembly, but in 1738 it became an independent colony and remained one until the Revolution made it a State.

Though the people in New Jersey at no time in its colonial history were allowed to choose their own governors, they were permitted to make their own laws and they received from Berkeley and Carteret many privileges which really amounted to a charter, though they were not one in name. Under royal governors the colony did not fare so well, still it prospered, and the liberal laws attracted many settlers from New York and other colonies who added to its wealth. The large manufactories for which New Jersey is now famed were at that time unknown, and most of the community then were farmers.

In 1746 the College of New Jersey was founded at Elizabeth, but was removed in 1757 to Princeton. It was the fourth American college to be established, following Yale and preceding the University of Pennsylvania.

9. *Pennsylvania.*

Like so many of the other colonies, Pennsylvania was founded as a refuge for those who had been

PENN'S ARRIVAL IN AMERICA.

persecuted for their religion in England, only this time it was neither Pilgrims nor Puritans, Baptists nor Roman Catholics who sought a home in the New World, but Quakers or members of the Society of Friends.

Their leader was William Penn. He was one of the most eminent Quakers in England, and was the son of a distinguished admiral in the British Navy, who had loaned a large sum of money to Charles II. to aid him in regaining his father's throne. Penn proposed to the King that in payment of this debt he should be given some land in America. This Charles was very willing to do, and in 1681 granted him the tract which now forms the State of Pennsylvania, a Latin word meaning "Penn's Woods."

Penn came over with a large body of settlers in 1682, and his first act was to buy the land needed for his colony from the Indians and to make a friendly treaty with them, which he took care should not afterwards be broken by the whites. His treatment of them was so just and so kind that the Indians always were on the best of terms with the Quakers, and would trust any one wearing their dress. The year after his arrival (1683) Penn laid out Philadelphia ("the city of brotherly love"), which soon became the largest city in this country and remained the largest until New York gained the lead in 1820.

In addition to the land obtained from King Charles, Penn bought (1682) from the Duke of York what is now the State of Delaware and which had been, like New Jersey, part of the New Netherlands. Settlements had already been made there and in some parts of Pennsylvania proper by the Swedes and Dutch as early as 1635, and by some English a little later. Penn did not disturb these settlers in their possessions; he even paid them for land occupied by them, which he desired as a site for Philadelphia.

Though the colony was intended as an asylum for Quakers, others were received into it as freely the attempts of the latter to again become King of England. But it was soon restored to him and remained in the posession of his family for nearly a hundred years, until in 1779 their rights were bought by the State for six hundred and fifty thousand dollars.

10. Delaware.

Delaware was first settled by the Swedes near the present city of Wilmington in 1638, and the name of New Sweden was given by them to the surrounding country, which they bought from the Indians. The Dutch considered it a part of the

PENN'S TREATY WITH THE INDIANS.

as were the Friends, and no one 'believing in Almighty God" was excluded or questioned further as to his faith. The governor was appointed by Penn, but the people elected the law-makers and chose most of their other officers. So excellent was the form of government adopted at the start, that scarcely any change was made in it until the colony became an independent State at the outbreak of the Revolution in 1776.

In 1692 Pennsylvania was for a short time taken away from Penn by William and Mary, because he was suspected of sympathizing with James II. in New Netherlands, and in 1655 compelled the Swedes to submit to their authority. When King Charles seized all the Dutch possessions in 1664 and gave them to his brother, the Duke of York, the latter soon sold (1682) Delaware to William Penn. From that time until the Revolution it formed part of Pennsylvania, though after 1703 it had a separate assembly, but not a separate governor. During its colonial history, it was known as "the Territories" or "the three lower counties on the Delaware," so called from the river on which they were situated and which took its name from Lord Delaware. When the colonies separated from Great Britain in 1776 it organized a government independent of Pennsylvania and so became one of the thirteen original States.

Under the rule of Penn and of his descendants it shared the mild, liberal government of the people of Pennsylvania. The occupation (farming) of the inhabitants of the two colonies was the same, and their history was uneventful but prosperous.

planted in 1664 by emigrants from Virginia on the Chowan River and named Albemarle, and the following year another settlement was established near Wilmington and called the Clarendon County colony. Both of these names were those of prominent proprietors of the grant.

The form of government adopted for Carolina was a peculiar one and unlike that of any of the other colonies. It was drawn up for the proprietors

PENN'S HOUSE.

11. *North Carolina.*

A hundred years passed after the failure of the French to settle at Port Royal before another attempt was made to colonize that part of our country. Then the English tried and succeeded.

In 1663 the territory now included in both Carolinas, Georgia and the northern half of Florida was given by the English sovereign to eight proprietors who retained the name of Carolina previously given it by the French as it honored their present King, Charles II., as much as it had the former French one, Charles IX. (The Latin word for Charles is "Carolus;" hence, "Carolina.")

Under these eight joint-owners a colony was

by the celebrated English philosopher, John Locke, and created a nobility of various degrees of rank (called barons, landgraves and caziques), who were to possess all the authority, leaving the people without any share in the government. This the settlers naturally did not like, so that the scheme, after a trial of twenty years, had to be abandoned.

Besides the colonies in Albemarle and Clarendon counties, other settlements were made, chiefly in the southern part of the grant. For a considerable time these were all under one government, but the distance between the northern and southern settlements was so great that it was finally thought best to separate them into two counties of the same province—North and South Carolina. Though these had different governors, they were still both under control of the same proprietors and were properly regarded as one colony until 1729, when a final separation was made and they became independent of each other. They then became royal colonies, the proprietors giving back the territory to the King on account of their inability to collect their rents from the settlers.

In none of the colonies was the population so scattered as in North Carolina, and few of them were so poor. But though it grew slowly it grew surely and soon became firmly established, and the people showed great independence and liberality. No religious persecution was allowed, and the attempt to adopt the Church of England as a state (or colonial) church was defeated in North Carolina while it succeeded in South Carolina. The governors sent from England to rule over North Carolina were among the worst that any of the colonies were afflicted with, and its colonial history consists almost entirely of a series of conflicts on the part of the people to defend their rights against the tyranny of the King's representatives.

12. South Carolina.

The first settlement in what is now South Carolina was made in 1670 on the Ashley River and became afterwards known as Old Charleston. Ten years later the settlement was removed to where the Cooper River unites with the Ashley and the foundations laid of the present city of Charleston. The colonists who in 1665 had settled in Clarendon County (North Carolina), but who had not prospered there, removed in a body to this new settlement, which also received a number of Huguenots (French Protestants), as well as some Dutch from New York who were discontented with the changes which followed its transfer to the English. Other settlements sprang up in South Carolina in addition to the one about Charleston, but that for a long time was the only town of any importance in the colony.

VIEW LOOKING UP THE DELAWARE RIVER.

Farming and hunting and the extraction of tar and turpentine from trees were the principal occupations of the North Carolinians. In South Carolina the production of rice was at first the great industry of its people, and like furs in New York and tobacco in Maryland and Virginia, rice in South Carolina was used in place of money. Later on, the cultivation of indigo was introduced and became even more important than rice. The raising and export to England of these two articles made South Carolina one of the richest of the thirteen colonies. Cotton, which afterwards became "king" throughout the South, was raised very little before the Revolutionary War, as there was no machinery then for cleaning it or separating the seeds from the fibre.

Until Georgia was settled South Carolina was exposed on her southern side to attacks from the Spaniards in Florida, and between 1702 and 1706 there was warfare between the settlements of the two different nations, during which St. Augustine was captured, but it did not remain long in the English hands, the Spaniards soon retaking it. South Carolina also had trouble with Indian allies of Florida, but with the aid of Virginia and Maryland she defeated them and finally broke their power so that they left her in peace.

Though the people of South Carolina in 1706 made the Church of England the religion of the colony, there was no persecution of those of a different belief. There was the same opposition in South Carolina on the part of the settlers to the payment of rents to the proprietors that there was in North Carolina, and it was this which caused the two Carolinas to be given back by their joint-owners to the King in 1729, and to their becoming from that time until 1776 separate royal colonies.

13. Georgia.

Georgia, the last of the thirteen colonies to be settled, had been part of the tract given to the proprietors of Carolina, and which they gave back to the English crown in 1729. No attempt to colonize it was made during the ownership of the proprietors, nor did South Carolina, after she became a separate royal colony, look upon it as a very valuable part of her territory. She was therefore quite willing to part with it when George II. in 1732 granted this land to James Oglethorpe and others as a home for poor people.

Oglethorpe was an officer in the English army who had become very much interested in the miserable state of the English poor, and who had devoted his life to doing whatever was in his power to raise their condition. Among his plans was founding a colony for them in America, where he thought they might succeed better than they had done in England. So he obtained a grant of this land from the King, and secured from Parliament a sum of money with which to start the enterprise.

The new colony was named Georgia in honor of King George, and the first settlement in it was made at Savannah in 1733 under the personal direction of Oglethorpe himself. Like the earliest Virginia settlers, the Savannah colonists were poor material for pioneers, comprising chiefly London tradesmen, who had failed in the effort to make a living in the Old World, and who were in every way unsuited to the task before them in the New World. A better class afterwards joined them, who somewhat improved and strengthened the colony, but it grew very slowly and remained the weakest, if not the poorest of the original colonies.

The government at first was placed by the King in the hands of twenty-one trustees, whose power was to last twenty-one years, but before that time expired, they gave back their authority to the King (1752), and Georgia, like most of the others, became a royal colony.

Oglethorpe followed Penn's policy in paying the Indians for the land used by his colonists, and this secured him the friendship of the Indians, who therefore gave the Georgia settlers very little trouble. Their nearness to Florida, however, often brought them into conflict with the Spaniards settled there, and for many years the two nations were almost at constant war, neither side gaining much advantage over the other.

After spending ten years in Georgia, Oglethorpe returned to England, where he lived long enough to see the independence of the colony he had established acknowledged by Great Britain.

CHAPTER V.

THE WHITES AND THE INDIANS.

BETWEEN the beginning of the settlement of the country at Jamestown in 1607 and the outbreak of the Revolutionary War in 1776 the number of white people in America had increased from one hundred to two and a half millions. By far the largest part of these were English, but by no means all. For besides the Dutch in New York, the Swedes in Delaware and in New Jersey, the French Huguenots in South Carolina, who have already been spoken of, there were scattered throughout the thirteen colonies many Germans, Scotch, Irish and people from other European countries, who, like the English, had come here to secure for themselves and for their children, greater freedom and better homes than they could have any hope of ever obtaining in crowded Europe.

The discomforts and sufferings of those who first came were very great. Only a few could afford to build any but the plainest and cheapest houses. Most of them had to be content with log-cabins, without floors. Many had only bark huts, like the wigwams made by the Indians, and some had to live in holes dug in the ground. Their furniture was of the simplest kind, benches, stools, tables and bedsteads being all home-made; for the number of colonists who were able to bring these things with them across the ocean was very small. Carpets were unknown and their place supplied with sand sprinkled upon the floor.

At first the settlements were all scattered along the coast, and were quite a distance apart. There were no roads between them, only bridle-paths and

MASSACRE OF SETTLERS.

Indian trails, and travelling from one to another was extremely difficult and dangerous. Journeys which we can now make in a few hours then took days and even weeks, and it was easier and safer to cross the ocean from America to England than to travel from New York to Boston.

All of this, however, gradually improved. As the settlements increased in number and in size, the distance between them grew smaller. Roads were made and bridges built, so that regular intercourse could be held between towns and villages and between the different colonies. And by the time the war of independence began, it was possible to journey through the entire range of settlements with some degree of comfort, if not with any great degree of speed.

With the growth in population and lapse of time, the wealth of the colonists also increased. They were able to build better houses than they first occupied; to give up the clothes made of leather which they first wore, for garments of cloth; and to surround themselves with many comforts and luxuries which at first they had been compelled to do without.

Though the colonists were still dependent upon England for the supply of many articles needed by them, and which could not be obtained in America, they amply paid for whatever they received with the tobacco, rice, indigo, furs and other valuable products raised by them. They became not only able to support themselves, to accumulate wealth and to pay the expenses of their town and colonial governments, but were also able to give money and ships to the King of England to aid him in carrying on his wars. All the colonies were not equally prosperous, nor were all the settlers in each colony equally well off, but they were on the whole all improving and constantly bettering their condition. Much of their wealth came from the labor of slaves, who, before the Revolution began, were to be found in all of the colonies.

During a considerable part of the one hundred and seventy years of colonial history, the whites and Indians were on terms of friendship. Some of the colonies, as Georgia, New Jersey and Pennsylvania, by their just and kind treatment of the natives, remained at peace with them throughout all this time. Others were less wise or less fortunate and suffered cruelly at their hands. The early settlers in these colonies did not dare to attend church unarmed. They carried their weapons to the cornfield and kept them within reach when they went to bed at night. Block-houses were built large enough to contain all the people in the settlement, to be used in case of an Indian rising, and sometimes an entire village would be enclosed with a stockade or wall, to shut out the common enemy.

The fault in these disturbances was sometimes on one side and sometimes on the other, but it was oftener with the whites than with the Indians. The earliest explorers and colonists found the natives peaceable, generous and friendly, but when they were ill-treated or thought themselves wrongly used, they became revengeful and horribly cruel. And many of the whites did ill-treat them. They seemed to think the Indians had no right to the land they were occupying when the whites came, or to their other property, and they did not scruple to seize whatever they wished. In revenge the Indians would kill the first colonists they met, whether they were the wrong-doers or not, and this would bring on a general Indian outbreak. The wise foresight of Penn, Oglethorpe and the founders of some of the other colonies, in strictly insisting at the outset that neither land nor anything else must be taken from the Indians without their consent or without full payment, saved their settlements from much suffering, which other colonies brought on themselves by showing less care for the rights of their Indian neighbors. Humanity and honesty proved the best policy with the Indians, as they have with other people.

Few of the Indian outbreaks deserve the name of wars or need to be even mentioned. They were usually very brief, and only a single village or a single colony would be concerned in them. Virginia, New York, Georgia and most of the other colonies suffered more or less from such risings, and there are few towns or cities in the United States, two hundred years old, whose history does not contain some account of Indian troubles.

Of the really serious difficulties with the Indians, by far the most important was the long series of wars in which the French settlers in Canada as well as the Indians were opposed to the English colonists. But before coming to this there were two purely Indian wars which require some mention: the Pequot War and King Philip's War.

The Pequots were a race of Indians living on the shores of Long Island Sound east of the Connecticut River. They had had some disagreement with Massachusetts, and to revenge themselves attacked and killed a number of Connecticut settlers. Connecticut, aided by Massachusetts, sent a body of soldiers against them, who, though at first unsuccessful, by the end of the year (1637) entirely destroyed the tribe, killing nearly nine hundred of their number in battle. Had it not been for the influence of Roger Williams in dissuading the Narragansetts from joining the Pequots, the result of the war might not have been so favorable to the whites.

In King Philip's War all of the New England colonies were concerned. It was brought about by a younger son of Massasoit, who had made the treaty with the Plymouth Pilgrims when they first landed, and who faithfully kept it during his long life. But he died in 1659, and his son (named by the whites King Philip), who then became chief of the Wampanoags, was of different temper from his father, and looked upon the growing settlements of the English with a jealous eye, fearing that in time they would entirely drive out the Indians. He visited the various tribes from Maine to the Hudson, and persuaded them all to unite in a league against the colonists.

This scheme or plot of Philip's was discovered by a converted native missionary and told to the magistrates of Plymouth. Not long afterwards the informer was found drowned. Thereupon the colonists seized three Wampanoag Indians and hung them upon suspicion of having committed the murder. This caused a war, for which the Indians had been already secretly preparing, to at once break out, and a number of towns in western Massachusetts were attacked at almost the same moment and their inhabitants killed.

All of the colonies in New England promptly united in defence, and the war thus begun lasted

ATTACK ON THE PEQUOT FORT.

for two years (1675-1677), during which six hundred settlers lost their lives in open battle and an unknown but probably much larger number in massacre and by starvation. Thirteen towns were destroyed and many more attacked and injured. The superior arms and better discipline of the whites at length proved too much for the Indians, who were driven back from point to point and finally were completely and overwhelmingly defeated. King Philip was killed and his son sold into slavery.

CHAPTER VI.

THE FRENCH AND INDIAN WARS.

THE French and Indian wars had their origin in difficulties and jealousies between the English and French settlers along the Mississippi River and in the Northwest, as Ohio and the region about it were then called. For while the English were busy in planting their colonies on the Atlantic coast, the French were not only extending their settlements along the St. Lawrence in Canada, but were also establishing themselves on the Mississippi River, and in northern New York, in Michigan, and at other points near the Canadian border in what is now the United States. They had obtained a grant of Louisiana (so named by them in honor of their King, Louis XIV.), and in 1718 founded the city of New Orleans, which soon became the most important point on the Mississippi. To secure the safety of these settlements they built a chain of forts, sixty in number, from New Orleans to Montreal.

All of this mattered very little to the English at first, for while their settlements were few and small they did not venture very far back from the coast. But as their colonies grew stronger and their population larger, they began to push into the wilderness, and this brought them into conflict with the French. The first difficulty between the two nationalities arose as early as 1689, and was followed by others at frequent intervals, until the final struggle was ended in favor of the English in 1763. These little wars usually had for their pretext European conflicts in progress at the time between France and England, and the names given to them are generally those of the English king or queen during whose reign they broke out. They really form but parts of one long war which had for its object the determination of the question which nation, the English or the French, was to rule North America.

Those earlier struggles, known as King William's War, Queen Anne's War, King George's War, etc., though they scarcely deserve such dignified names, resulted in no decided gain to either side, the French perhaps profiting a little more than the English. They were of slight importance in them-

NEW ORLEANS.

selves, but they gradually led up to something which was of real importance and which is known in American history as *the* French and Indian War.

Unlike the minor wars which preceded this final contest between the settlers of these two nations, the French and Indian War originated on this continent and at a time when the parent countries in Europe were at peace with each other. Its cause may be found in the attempt which was made by the English to open up and settle the western lands on a larger scale than had ever before been tried.

About the middle of the last century some London merchants united with a number of Virginia planters to form the Ohio Company, which bought a large tract of land west of the Alleghany Mountains with a view to inducing settlers to move there.

As soon as this Company began operations by sending out surveyors and traders and by making roads for emigrants, the French colonists became alarmed, justly fearing if the English succeeded in

UNLOADING A COTTON STEAMER AT NEW ORLEANS.

settling that region as extensively as they planned that the French would soon be obliged to entirely withdraw from the interior of the continent and to content themselves with their Canadian possessions. To prevent this and to secure for themselves the land desired by the Ohio Company, the French in 1753 put up a strong fort where the city of Erie now stands, and prepared to build other forts extending from that point to the Ohio River. Virginia claimed this land as part of her territory and the governor of the colony sent George Washington, then only twenty-two years old, but who had already acquired distinction on the frontier as a surveyor, to protest against this action of the French. Though he was received with civility and courtesy, Washington did not succeed in his mission and had to return with the refusal of the French commander to either give up the fort or to leave the disputed territory.

During Washington's absence Virginia had raised a body of four hundred soldiers, and she promptly replied to this message by sending him back at the head of this force to protect a fort which the Ohio Company was building on the site of the city of Pittsburg. But the French were before him and had seized and strengthened the fort, which they then named Fort Du Quesne, before he could get there. They then hastened on to attack Washington, who defeated their advance guard,

SCENE ON THE OHIO RIVER.

but who thought it wiser to fall back before the main body of the French, as it greatly exceeded in numbers his force. He retired to a small fort (named by him Fort Necessity) near Fort Du Quesne, and there (on July 4, 1754) he surrendered to the French on the condition that he and his soldiers might return to Virginia.

In the contest that followed, the French received very valuable aid from their Indian allies, as indeed they had all acted together, but they knew that this western land was necessary for the growth of their country and that all were equally interested in keeping out the French. England and France were at first disposed to let the colonists fight it out by themselves, but they soon became involved in one of their frequent wars with each other in Europe and so in self-defence sent troops to the aid of their settlers in America.

ARRIVAL OF INDIAN AUXILIARIES AT FORT DU QUESNE.

they had in their earlier difficulties with the English. It was this which gave it the name of the French and Indian War. The French treatment of the Indians had been much more friendly than that of the English; they had regarded them more as equals, had shown them greater kindness in every way, and so the Indians were far more willing to assist the French than they were to help the English.

All the colonies rallied to the assistance of Virginia and voted arms, money and men to fight the French. It was the first time in their history that

At first the English were unsuccessful, for though they drove the French out of Nova Scotia and defeated a body of French and Indians in northern New York near Lake George, they were badly beaten in an attempt to capture Fort Du Quesne, and their commander, General Braddock, and half his force were killed. Washington served as an aide to Braddock in this campaign, and by his skill and coolness checked the pursuit of the enemy after the defeat and brought the survivors back to Virginia. This was in 1755, and for two years more the Eng-

THE FRENCH AND INDIAN WARS.

lish did not do much better, for though they kept attacking the French at many points they did not succeed in gaining possession of the coveted country, ment to lead the colonial troops. The French soldiers were a smaller body of men, but they were better organized and had for their commander a brill-

BRADDOCK'S FORCES SURPRISED BY AN AMBUSCADE.

try, but even lost the few forts they had built along the border between Canada and New York.

The chief cause of these disasters was the poor quality of the officers sent by the British Government iant general (Montcalm), who with his few soldiers was more than a match for his opponents with their larger forces. In time England realized her mistake, and by 1758 matters improved. More able

GENERAL MONTCALM.

commanders were sent to America, who, instead of frittering away their strength in a multitude of little and trifling engagements, attacked three points that were of real importance, and two of these they captured. These were Louisburg on Cape Breton Island and Fort Du Quesne, which was then renamed Fort Pitt in honor of the Prime Minister of Great Britain, William Pitt. Ticonderoga (in New York), the third point of attack, was defended by Montcalm in person, and here the English were less fortunate, for though they tried again and again, Montcalm each time drove them back, and at length they had to retire, leaving fifteen hundred of their men dead behind them. Though they did not take Ticonderoga, the English did capture Fort Frontenac (where the Canadian city of Kingston now stands) and drove the French out of northwestern New York.

From this time on the successes of the English were almost continuous, and the capture of Quebec in 1759 virtually ended the war, for after that the French forts surrendered as fast as the English appeared before them to demand it. Montcalm lost his life in battle on the Plains of Abraham before Quebec, as did also his English opponent, General Wolfe. The dying words of each showed the characters of the two men. When Montcalm was told that he must die, he said: "So much the better, I shall not live to see the surrender of Quebec." Wolfe was mortally wounded when word was brought to him that the battle was won: "Then I die happy," he said.

By the close of 1760 Montreal and all the other American possessions of the French were in the hands of the English, and the French troops had returned to France. But though hostilities had ceased in this country, they did not end in Europe until 1763, when a treaty of peace was signed by the three countries (Spain had assisted France in Europe) by which France gave up to Great Britain all of her territory in America east of the Mississippi and to Spain what lay west of that river. From Spain England obtained Florida, in exchange for Havana. The district granted Spain extended from the Mississippi to the Rocky Mountains, and the name of Louisiana given it by the French was retained by Spain. France bought it back from Spain in 1800 and in 1803 sold it to the United States.

The French and Indian War did this great service for the colonists: it taught them to act together and in unison. It also gave them experience in warfare and in military matters. The colonial soldiers fighting by the side of British troops gained both knowledge and confidence in themselves, and they and their officers learnt many a valuable lesson which a dozen years later they put to good use in the Revolutionary War.

GENERAL WOLFE.

CHAPTER VII.

SEPARATION FROM ENGLAND.

How many boys and girls have ever noticed in looking at the American flag that it always has just thirteen stripes? And how many know that these stripes represent the thirteen colonies whose settlement you have been reading about? These were the first States, and though others have since come into the Union whose territory is larger, whose population is greater, and which are richer and perhaps more enterprising than were some of these original colonies, yet the names of these thirteen should always be gratefully remembered by every American, for it was their self-denial, courage and perseverance which in the first place colonized the country, and in the second place freed it and made of it the Union.

We have seen that each of these colonies had something different about it from the others. New York was Dutch, Pennsylvania was Quaker, Maryland was Catholic, New Jersey Swedish, Massachusetts Puritan, and Virginia Cavalier. Even where the nationality and the religion were the same a difference in the wealth of the settlers or in their character soon made itself apparent in differences in the laws and customs of the colonies, and Massachusetts was not the same as Connecticut or North Carolina the same as South Carolina. But whatever their differences might be they were alike in one respect: they were all jealous of their rights; none of them liked English interference in their affairs; and each of them preferred to make its own laws and to govern itself rather than to be ruled by the British King or by the British Parliament.

This showed itself very early in their history when King James II., who seemed to believe that the people neither in England nor America had any rights which he was bound to respect, attempted to take away the charters which had already been given the colonies and sent over Sir Edmond Andros to govern New England and New York without regard to law. For three years (1686–1689) the people opposed and resisted him every way they could, and at length seized him by force and sent him back to London. Some of the other governors in New York and North Carolina fared no better; the people rose in arms and compelled them to

ANDROS A PRISONER IN BOSTON.
(From Butterworth's "Young Folks' History of the United States.")

leave the country. In Virginia as well there was open rebellion, and the colonies were few in number where there was not more or less resistance at times to the royal authority.

From the outset the British government showed but little sympathy with the colonists, and seemed more disposed to hinder than to help them. They had scarcely got a start when the Navigation Laws were passed (1651) which forbade the settlers from trading with any other country than England or from permitting the vessels of any other nation to enter American ports. The colonists found these laws very oppressive and they were a constant source of grievance against the mother country. They were not, however, always strictly enforced, and the colonists managed by bribery and smuggling for the most part to evade them. Other laws prohibiting the manufacture of certain articles in America were almost as burdensome as the Navigation Laws, and were disregarded in much the same way.

Still, notwithstanding the tyrannical governors who at times were sent over to rule them, and notwithstanding what they felt to be the injustice of the Navigation and Manufacturing Laws, the colonists on the whole were loyal to England and would probably have had no thought of revolting when they did, had not Great Britain begun to apply these laws with a vigor never before displayed, besides adopting other measures even more distasteful to the colonies.

For after the French and Indian Wars England seemed to suddenly wake to the growing size, wealth and importance of the settlements and to become uneasy at the liberty and freedom allowed them. She seemed to fear that unless steps were taken to check their progress towards self-rule they would soon wish to be entirely independent of her and to set up a separate government of their own. The feeling of indifference she had shown before disappeared, and in its place appeared a lively anxiety to restrain and control them while there was yet time. With this end in view she determined to carry out the Navigation Laws to the letter and also to obtain money from the colonists by taxation.

Heretofore, while the colonies had very willingly taxed themselves to support the governors sent to them and for the administration of their own laws, they had not been called upon to pay any money to England, and they received with indignation this demand that they should help bear the expenses of a distant government in which they had no voice either as to how the money was to be raised or how it was to be spent. The cry of "no taxation without representation" was at once raised, and the colonists resolved to pay no tax levied by Great Britain.

The first test of their resolution came in 1765, when Parliament passed the Stamp Act, which required that all newspapers, almanacs, marriage certificates and legal documents of every description should have on them stamps furnished by the English government and which must be bought from agents appointed to sell them in the colonies. The Americans acted quickly. As soon as the stamps arrived they were seized by mobs and burned, the stamp-officers were forced to resign their positions, and on the day appointed for the law to go into effect not a stamp could be found in the colonies. The Stamp Act was a failure and in the following year it was repealed.

But in abandoning this particular tax the British government had no thought of giving up its claim to the right to tax, and soon duties (as they are

THE STAMP ACT.

SEPARATION FROM ENGLAND.

called) were imposed upon a number of articles imported to the colonies, as tea, glass, paper, paints and other things. These duties the colonists refused to pay, and agreed among themselves to purchase nothing from England while she continued her attempt to tax them. In the meantime the Navigation and Manufacturing Laws were enforced with the greatest severity, and soldiers were sent from England to aid the civil authorities in detecting and arresting smugglers and other violators of these laws, and these soldiers the colonists were required to shelter and feed. New York and Boston, to their credit be it said, refused to do this, and in those places other provision had to be made for these soldiers.

The colonists had now entered upon a struggle with Great Britain which they meant to be peaceable, and which was peaceable at first, but which tended all the time towards warfare. The attempts of revenue officers to seize smuggled goods and vessels in which the goods had been brought were resisted and often led to street fights. The vast majority of the Americans were united in their resolution to oppose by every means in their power foreign taxation; but there were a few adherents of the mother-country. They were called Tories; their opponents were named Whigs, or "Sons of Liberty,"

as many of them delighted to call themselves. As the contest went on, each side grew more bitter and exasperated, Parliament in its determination to find some way by which the colonists would be forced to pay a tax, and the Americans in their resolution that nothing should induce them to pay one penny.

In 1770 Parliament changed its tactics and tried to obtain by a trick what it had before been unable to secure openly. It took off the tax from everything but tea, and on that it reduced the duty to three pence (six cents) a pound. Then it arranged with London merchants to sell the tea in the colonies at three pence a pound less than it was sold for in England. By this device the tea with the tax added to its price would cost the colonists no more than they would have to pay for it in England. But it was the principle of taxation, not the amount, that the Americans were struggling against, and they met this move as promptly as they had the attempt to impose stamps upon them. At Philadelphia and some other places they sent the ships back to London with all the tea on board. At Charleston the tea was placed (the chests unopened) in cellars, where the dampness soon ruined it. At Boston a number of citizens dressed themselves as Indians and in an orderly but resolute way proceeded to the ships in

DESTROYING THE TEA IN BOSTON HARBOR.

the harbor and threw all the tea overboard. By one means or other the tea was gotten rid of at every place it had been sent to, and Parliament was once more thwarted in its plans to obtain money from the colonies.

The action of the "Boston Tea-Party" especially angered the English government and in punishment it closed the port of Boston by forbidding all vessels either to enter it or to leave it. Parliament also took away from the people of Massachusetts their right to make their own laws. The other colonies all sided with Massachusetts in her opposition to England, and the effect of these measures was only to strengthen still more the bond of colonial union. This sentiment was further increased by the passage of other laws by Parliament at the same time that those affecting Boston and Massachusetts were adopted, one of which ordered that all Americans accused of murder in resisting English laws should be sent to Great Britain for trial. The execution of these and other hateful acts was given to the British troops already in the colonies and the number of which was now considerably increased.

The Americans by this time had become thoroughly roused and the excitement ran high. Each town felt that it might receive the same treatment as Boston, each colony knew that its liberties were no more safe than those of Massachusetts. There was a general demand for a Continental Congress, and one accordingly was chosen by the people and met in Philadelphia in September, 1774. Georgia was the only colony which did not send delegates, and she was only prevented from doing so by her governor.

CHAPTER VIII.

THE MINUTE-MEN AT LEXINGTON AND AT BUNKER HILL.

THREE things of importance were done by this first Continental Congress, and the chief of these three was the preparation of two addresses, one to the people of Great Britain and one to King George, in which were recited the many wrongs which Parliament had inflicted (or had attempted to inflict) upon the Americans, and which again asserted the right of the colonists to govern themselves and not to be taxed without their own consent. Next it drew up an agreement neither to buy anything from England nor to sell anything to her, nor to transact business of any kind with her until Parliament repealed the laws which had been passed against the colonies. Copies of this agreement were sent into every town and village in America and were signed by the people everywhere. Lastly it promised to aid Massachusetts with troops from the other colonies if they should be needed in her resistance to Great Britain's attempt to force her into submission. Important as these three acts were, what was of far more importance was the evidence furnished by the meeting of the Congress itself that the colonies were thoroughly united in their determination to do everything in their power to maintain what they knew to be their rights.

Though the language of the Continental Congress was mild, its attitude was firm and unyielding, and every one felt that open war must soon come, and

BRITISH GRENADIER.

MINUTE-MAN.

THE MINUTE-MEN AT LEXINGTON AND AT BUNKER HILL.   45

every one began to prepare for it. Massachusetts, it was plain, would be the first battle-ground, and there was the greatest activity—the people collecting and storing weapons, powder and shot, and the English governor (Gage) increasing the number of his soldiers and defending his position by erecting fortifications around Boston.

The first blow was soon struck. Gage learned from spies, employed by him to find out what the colonists were doing, that about twenty miles from Boston, at Concord, the Americans had gathered together a quantity of ammunition and supplies. He determined to destroy these and sent for the purpose a body of eight hundred soldiers with orders to proceed as secretly as possible in order to surprise those in charge of the stores.

But friends in Boston discovered the plan just before the party started and sent word by Paul Revere to the patriots, so that when at daybreak on the morning of April 19, 1775, the British soldiers entered Lexington on the road to Concord they were met by some seventy "minute-

BATTLE OF LEXINGTON.

men," as the colonial militia were called from their being always ready on an instant's notice to take up their arms. The English opened fire and the Americans returned it, but after exchanging a few shots the Americans retired with eight of their men dead and a number of others wounded. The British then proceeded to Concord, destroyed the supplies collected there and started back towards Boston.

But the Americans had not been idle while the English were accomplishing their work of destruction. Warned by church-bell and messenger the whole country round about had become ablaze, and minute-men hurried from every quarter to meet the enemy on its return. At first the British march was orderly and the fire from the patriots was steadily and coolly returned, but as the number of the minute-men increased and from every point on the road affording the least shelter there was poured upon the English a constant stream of deadly shot, they lost their nerve and were chased by the colonists into Lexington on a run. There they were reinforced by a fresh body of nine hundred soldiers whom Gage had sent to their relief and who were provided with cannon, and under their protection they at last reached Boston, pursued the whole distance by the minute-men. The total number of Americans engaged was but four hundred, of whom they lost eighty-eight. The killed, wounded and missing among the English numbered two hundred and seventy odd.

CHRIST CHURCH (WHERE THE SIGNAL LANTERN WAS DISPLAYED).

The die was cast. The war was begun. From it a nation was to emerge destined to become the freest, wealthiest and probably in time the largest and most powerful on the face of the globe. An experiment in self-government was to be tried on a scale never before attempted and with results for good no man could have imagined possible. Could they who laid down their lives at Lexington have foreseen the rich harvests their children were to reap they would have counted their own sacrifice as nothing.

The minute-men who had pursued the English from Concord and from Lexington were speedily joined by others from the several New England colonies, and soon twenty thousand surrounded Boston and were besieging it on every side excepting that towards the sea. Within the city the British forces were also increased until there were ten thousand men under command of Generals Howe, Clinton and Burgoyne, who had come to the assistance of Governor Gage. The ten thousand English soldiers were well-armed, disciplined, experienced veterans; their twenty thousand opponents were for the most part raw farmers, with no knowledge of the art of war, untrained, poorly supplied with weapons, with no cannon and with little food. The greater number of the Americans was thus offset by the greater efficiency of their enemy.

North of Boston are two hills, Bunker and Breed's, the first of which the Americans decided to fortify. By mistake the party sent under Colonel Prescott to do this selected Breed's Hill, which was nearer to Boston than Bunker Hill. They worked at night as silently and as rapidly as possible and by daybreak, when the British discovered what was going on, had thrown up a long line of entrenchments facing Boston. The English

PAUL REVERE.

THE BATTLE OF BUNKER HILL.

men-of-war in the harbor at once began to bombard these fortifications, but without preventing the Americans from continuing their work of strengthening their position. Then three thousand soldiers were sent to dislodge the workmen and to capture the place. The fifteen hundred minute-men, without offering to fire a shot, calmly watched their assailants march up the Hill, while from every housetop in the city multitudes anxiously looked on, wondering if the undisciplined Yankee farmers

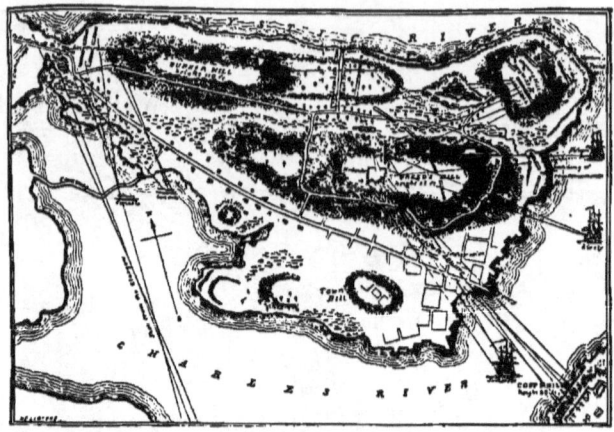

PLAN OF BATTLE OF BUNKER HILL.

would stand a single round from their seasoned and battle-tried opponents. Not until the British were within one hundred and fifty feet of the breastworks was this question answered, and then there was a flash of fire from the entrenchments, part of the attacking column fell, and the rest, routed, were flying back.

Urged on by their officers they turned at the foot of the Hill to renew the assault. The Americans waited in the same silence as before until the English were close at hand and again with their fatal fire drove them down the Hill. Once more the British re-formed and for the third time ascended the Hill to attempt the capture. This time they succeeded, for the Americans had exhausted their ammunition and, although they fought desperately with stones and used their guns as clubs, the British bayonets were too much for them and they were obliged to retreat, leaving the fortifications they had so gallantly defended in the hands of the enemy.

This Battle of Bunker Hill, as it has always been called and probably always will be, was fought on June 17, 1775, and was of the greatest service to the colonial cause in showing that Continental troops, unused to war as they were, could stand fire and were not afraid to meet veterans in battle. It gave the Americans a confidence in themselves at the start which even in their worst reverses they never afterwards lost.

MONUMENT AT BUNKER HILL.

CHAPTER IX.

WASHINGTON IN COMMAND.

GEORGE WASHINGTON.

WHILE the siege of Boston was in progress and before the Battle of Bunker Hill took place. Congress met again (May 10, 1775) at Philadelphia and, still asserting its loyalty to the King, declared that as Parliament had begun the war upon the colonies they would defend themselves until their rights and liberties were respected. Provision was made for raising troops in addition to those around Boston, the whole to form a Continental Army of which George Washington was appointed Commander-in-Chief. A system of taxation was also adopted and laws passed for the government of the country as long as the trouble with England lasted.

Two weeks after the Battle of Bunker Hill Washington arrived at the camp before Boston and began his task of drilling the besiegers into an effective body of soldiers. While he was thus busy other Americans were planning an invasion of Canada. Shortly after the Lexington fight, Ticonderoga had been captured by some Connecticut militia under Ethan Allen and Benedict Arnold, and a day or two later Crown Point also fell into their hands and with it a large number of cannon and a quantity of powder—two things greatly needed by the young colonial army. The possession of these two places left the way clear through New York to Canada. Accordingly, in the latter part of the summer of 1775 two parties set out, one under Generals Montgomery and Schuyler by way of Lake Champlain, and the other under Benedict Arnold which was to force its way through the Maine wilderness and join the first division in front of Quebec. The expedition was a failure, for though Montreal was taken, Quebec was too strong for the American attack, and after spending the winter in a fruitless effort to capture the city, Arnold, who by the illness of Schuyler and death of Montgomery had risen to the chief command, was forced in the spring of 1776 to abandon the attempt and to leave Canada, what it has since remained, an English possession.

By March, 1776, Washington had got his army into better shape than he found it when he was made its general, and was ready to repeat the attempt which had failed the previous June. He had kept the British closely confined to Boston all winter and now thought it time to drive them out. Selecting a hill to the south of the city, called Dorchester Heights, he took possession of it at night and, aid-

GEORGE III.

QUEBEC, SHOWING THE CITADEL.

fighting the English Parliament and not the King. But matters could not go on in that way much longer, and early in 1776 the question of separation from Great Britain began to be more generally considered and discussed than it had been before. Throughout the quarrel King George III. had constantly sided with Parliament and had approved all its measures aimed at the injury of the Americans. He displayed as much bitter feeling against them as did any of his subjects. When the news of the battle of Bunker Hill reached

ed by a storm, had it strongly fortified before the English commander in Boston, General Howe, was able to attack it.

As the guns from Dorchester Heights completely commanded the city, Howe concluded it best to leave, and on March 17, 1776, set sail for Halifax, and the Americans entered Boston. No further events of importance occurred in Massachusetts during the Revolution, and in fact all of New England was from this time forth comparatively free from the British.

Thus far the colonies had been

QUEBEC.

WASHINGTON IN COMMAND.

England, he at once arranged to send twenty-five thousand more troops to conquer the "rebels" as he called them, among whom were a large number of Hessians, said to be the most cruel and inhuman of hireling soldiers. He ordered that all trade with the colonies be stopped and authorized their merchant ships to be seized and destroyed by any one wherever found. With his assent a number of towns on the coast were bombarded and ruined.

These actions at length had their natural effect in destroying the feelings of personal loyalty which had hitherto influenced the Americans, and caused them to regard the King as no less their enemy than were his ministers. They were forced to abandon all hope of obtaining redress from him, as they had before given up hope of securing it from Parliament. Their thoughts thereupon turned towards a complete separation from the mother-country.

The first step towards independence was taken by the colonies themselves on the advice of the Continental Congress, and consisted of the formation of State governments in place of the colonial ones which had already been overturned by the disagreement with Great Britain. This was done in May and June, 1776, and after that date the word "colony" was no longer used, the word "State" taking its place. The next step followed immediately; Virginia took the lead in directing her delegates in Congress to vote for independence and the other States were not slow in seconding her action. A committee was appointed by Congress to draw up suitable resolutions and the Declaration of Independence prepared by that Committee was adopted on July 4, 1776, and the United States became one of the nations of the world.

INDEPENDENCE HALL, PHILADELPHIA.

INTERIOR OF INDEPENDENCE HALL IN 1889.

Immediately after the British sailed from Boston Washington hastened to New York and began to collect an army and to fortify the city. He suc-

52   HISTORY OF THE UNITED STATES.

ceeded in getting together some twenty thousand men, but like those he found at Boston they were poorly armed and without experience in war. Gen. August 27, 1776, attacked a post of five thousand Americans whom Washington had stationed near Brooklyn, then a small village. The Americans

FAC-SIMILE OF THE SIGNATURES TO THE DECLARATION OF INDEPENDENCE.

Howe had come from Halifax to Staten Island and his force had been increased to thirty thousand practised soldiers. Taking with him about half of his men, Howe crossed over to Long Island and on were utterly defeated and nearly half of their number slain and taken prisoners. The remainder took refuge in a fort which had been erected in Brooklyn, and two days later, under cover of a fog, were

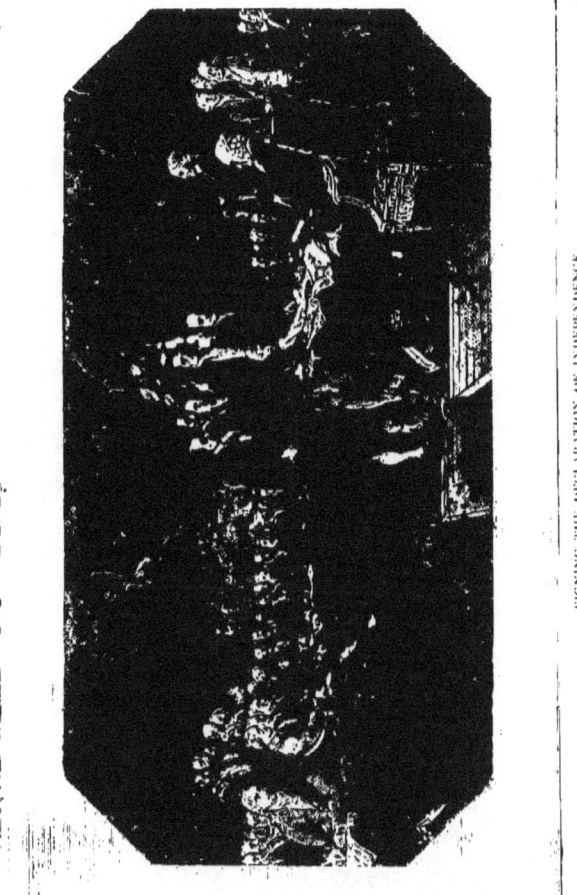

SIGNING THE DECLARATION OF INDEPENDENCE.

WASHINGTON READING THE DECLARATION OF INDEPENDENCE TO THE ARMY.

Leaving Gen. Charles Lee in command at that point, Washington crossed the Hudson with five thousand of his men and was followed by the British under Lord Cornwallis, who gradually drove the Americans across New Jersey to the Delaware River. This they crossed in open boats among cakes of floating ice (it was now December), but the exposure, the rapid retreat and the privations they brought by Washington to New York. Howe followed him, and Washington, making only a show of resistance, retreated to the hills near Peekskill.

GENERAL CHARLES LEE.

WASHINGTON CROSSING THE DELAWARE

suffered reduced the number of Washington's soldiers to three thousand, and the English felt confident that, as soon as the river froze over so that they could cross in safety, they could overtake Washington and by again defeating him end the war.

But Washington had a surprise in store for them. Selecting twenty-five hundred of his best men, on the night of Christmas, 1776, he secretly recrossed the Delaware and by daylight had surrounded the city of Trenton, whose entire garrison consisting of a thousand Hessians were captured with the loss of only four Americans. Hurrying with his prisoners to Philadelphia he left them there and at once returned to Trenton. The British forces from all parts of New Jersey quickly gathered at Trenton, and for the moment it looked as though Washington had allowed himself to be entrapped between the enemy on the one side and the river on the other. But he was equal to the emergency. Breaking camp at the dead of night he skirted the English encampment and marching to Princeton attacked and defeated three regiments stationed there and escaped to the mountains about Morristown in northern New Jersey, where Cornwallis, who had started in pursuit, did not think it best to follow him.

CHAPTER X.

THE LOSS OF PHILADELPHIA AND THE VICTORY AT SARATOGA.

DURING the third year of the war, 1777, the two events of most importance were the capture of Philadelphia by the British and the defeat of Burgoyne by the Americans. Scarcely less notable was the addition to the Revolutionary army of a number of European officers, who volunteered their services to Washington through sympathy with the American cause. Of these the most distinguished were the Marquis de la Fayette, who secretly fitted out a ship and sailed to America against the orders of the French government; Baron de Kalb, a German nobleman of distinction, and two Polish patriots, Kosciusko and Pulaski. Another very valuable accession was made the following year in the person of Baron von Steuben, who was of great service in improving the tactics of the republican army.

The opening of 1777 found the Americans strongly entrenched at Morristown in New Jersey and at Peekskill on the Hudson, from both of which positions the British were anxious to dislodge them, as well as to seize Philadelphia, then the largest city in the country. Fearing to attack Philadelphia directly by marching his soldiers across New Jersey in face of the American army, Howe sailed in July with eighteen thousand men from Staten Island without letting it be known where he was bound, and Washington was compelled to wait in New Jersey until he learned that the vessels had

VIEW OF WASHINGTON'S QUARTERS AT MORRISTOWN.

been seen in Chesapeake Bay. As this showed without doubt that Philadelphia was the object of the expedition, Washington hastened to the defence of the city, but only to be twice defeated, at Brandywine and Germantown (September and October, 1777), and Philadelphia fell into the hands of the British.

Congress had fled from Philadelphia before it was captured by Howe, and after his defeats Washington moved his army to Valley Forge, a small place on the Schuylkill, where he was near enough

GENERAL GATES.

to Philadelphia to attack the English if they left the city. Here the Americans passed the winter of 1777-78, suffering every manner of hardship from the cold, poorly housed, badly clad, with scanty food, and many of them with no boots or shoes to protect their bare feet from the snow and ice. But through all the horrors of that dismal season Washington did not despair. Patient, hopeful and confident in their final success, he held up the courage of his men, and was firm in his refusal to leave the point from which in the end he thought he could most injure the enemy. And despite the miseries of Washington's army, the American prospects were much brighter than they had been a year before—thanks to Schuyler and Gates in New York, whose victories over Burgoyne were far more important than Washington's ill-success in Pennsylvania.

The English greatly desired to gain control of the Hudson River, both because it would shut off New England from the rest of the country and because it was the easiest and most direct road to Canada. As the American position at Peekskill was too strong to be taken from the south, they determined to attempt it from the north; and so about the time that Washington was hastening to the defence of Philadelphia a British army of ten thousand men was moving from Canada under command of Sir Edward Burgoyne. Opposed to him was Gen. Schuyler with some five thousand men. Ticonderoga was easily captured by Burgoyne, and Schuyler fell back before him towards Albany, destroying bridges and blocking up the road behind him as he proceeded. At the mouth of the Mohawk River, where it unites with the Hudson, both armies came to a halt, Schuyler awaiting the aid of more troops, and Burgoyne hesitating to attack the Americans in their strong position on the river islands where they had camped.

During the pause which followed, meant by Burgoyne to be a very brief one, but which proved in the end a fatal one to him, he sent out two expeditions, one to the west to take Fort Schuyler on the site of the present city of Rome (New York), and one to the east to attack Bennington (Vermont). The first was defeated by Benedict Arnold and driven into Canada. The other suffered as severely at the hands of Col. Stark, whose short and famous speech to his men before the battle: "There they are, boys; we must beat them to-day or this night Mollie Stark's a widow," will not soon be forgotten.

The British loss in these two engagements weakened Burgoyne most seriously, while the American force against him had in the mean time been strengthened by the arrival of fresh troops sent to its assistance by Congress. Prevented from retreating by the militia which had now closed up his rear, he crossed to the west bank of the Hudson with the intention of descending the river and pushing his way through the American lines. In this he was checked by Gates, to whom Congress had given the command in place of Schuyler, and who, though he did not in the two battles of Bemis Heights and Stillwater succeed in driving the English from the field, yet so hemmed them in that they soon could neither advance nor recede. Burgoyne tried to hold his men together until Clinton, who he knew was on his way from New York, could arrive with reinforcements, but he was without provisions, his force had become reduced to six thousand men who were worn out with hunger and fatigue, and at last, on October 17, 1777, he surrendered to Gates at Saratoga.

Gates not only reaped the fruit of Schuyler's well-planned campaign, but he took all the credit of the result, and was the hero of the hour. The gloom which had rested upon the country in consequence of the loss of Philadelphia and Washington's reverses in Pennsylvania lifted, and so great was the exultation and so popular was the victor that an effort was even made in Congress to deprive Washington of the chief command of the Continental Army and to give it to Gates. Happily for the republic it failed. Washington retained the command that he alone in the difficulties of the time was fitted to hold, and in the course of a few years more brought the war to a successful close.

GENERAL BURGOYNE.

CHAPTER XI.

AID FROM FRANCE.

BESIDES increasing the confidence of the patriots in their cause and removing the danger of any further attempt at an invasion from Canada, Burgoyne's defeat was of especial value to the Americans in securing for them the open aid of France in continuing the war. Her long enmity with England had already insured them her private sympathy and some secret help. But though she rejoiced when by the adoption of the Declaration of Independence the United States separated themselves from Great Britain, she feared at first that they would not be equal to the task they had assumed, and that if she became their ally the chief burden of the contest would fall upon her. The Saratoga victory lessened this fear and proved that the Americans would bear their full share in any war to which they were a party. She was, therefore, now willing to become publicly known as their friend, and to enter into an alliance with them. Thanks mainly to Benjamin Franklin, who was the American agent in Paris throughout the Revolution, and who did much to shape public opinion there favorably to his country, a treaty was signed early in 1778 by which France agreed to send four thousand soldiers and sixteen ships of war to the assistance of the Americans.

This put a different face upon the war, and England became quite willing to grant to the United States all that she had previously refused them, and offered them freedom from taxation and representation in Parliament if they would give up the French alliance and join her in a war upon her old enemy. This the Americans declined to do. They neither wished to throw off their new friends nor to connect themselves again with Great Britain. Nothing but absolute independence would now content them.

The benefits from the French treaty proved to be less in the troops and ships sent to this country, which until the closing acts of the war were of little real aid, than in the money and supplies loaned by France to Congress. For these were the great needs of the time. The government, hastily formed when the war first broke out, and which consisted only of the Continental Congress, was a very imperfect one and with very indefinite powers, and it had great difficulty in obtaining money to pay the soldiers and to buy necessary supplies, so that the loans from France were of the greatest service to the Americans in aiding them to carry on the war. Another important result of the treaty was the European war it caused between France and Spain on the one side and Great Britain on the other, and this helped the Americans by preventing England from devoting so much attention to this country. All of these things combined made the assistance of France at this time extremely valuable to the Revolutionists, for without it the war would undoubtedly have lasted many more years than it did.

When the news of the formation of the French alliance reached Philadelphia, General Clinton, who had succeeded Howe in the command, decided to withdraw to New York in order to strengthen the British forces there as much as possible before the arrival of the expected French fleet. Washington, still encamped at Valley Forge, awaiting this opportunity, hastened after him in the hope of detaining him in New Jersey until the French should come. At Monmouth the two armies met and fought, but darkness came upon them before any decisive result was reached, and during the night Clinton succeeded in drawing off his men to New York. Had it not been for what was afterwards thought to be treachery on the part of Gen. Charles Lee in retreating when he had been ordered to attack, Washington might have won the battle. Lee was second in command, and at the outbreak of the war was regarded as one of the most brilliant officers on our side. For his conduct at Monmouth, followed by insolence to Washington, he was dismissed from the service.

Clinton transferred his forces from Philadelphia to New York in June, 1778. In July the French arrived, but their larger vessels were unable to enter the harbor of New York, so that the attack upon that city was abandoned, and the French sailed to the West Indies to defend their possessions among those islands. Washington, after the battle of Monmouth, resumed his old position on the Hudson near Peekskill, with a line extending

SIR HENRY CLINTON.

across to Morristown, ready to meet the British if they ventured towards New England, Philadelphia, or Camden—the three points most likely to be the objects of any land-attack from New York. This position he maintained for three years, carefully watching every sign of movement of the enemy, and by his vigilance preventing their doing anything of moment either in the Middle States or in New England. During the remainder of the war the principal events took place in the South.

CHAPTER XII.

THE WAR IN THE SOUTH AND ARNOLD'S TREASON.

THE close of the year 1778 saw the first of the operations in the South, when an expedition sent by Clinton (by sea) captured Savannah. Augusta soon followed, and before long all of Georgia was overrun by British troops from New York and Florida. As yet the United States had practically no navy, and the French war vessels were rarely at hand when needed, so that no matter how strong Washington's land-blockade around New York might be, he was without any means of preventing Clinton from shipping his men to whatever port in the country he desired.

Congress had built a few naval vessels, but they had either been captured by the English or were too small to contend against the British frigates. A little later on a few ships were obtained from France, and fitted out as American men-of-war. One of these, named the "Bonhomme Richard," under command of Paul Jones, met two frigates off the northeastern coast of England (Sept., 1779), and there was fought one of the most notable battles in naval history. Jones lashed his ship to the "Serapis" (one of the frigates), and a hand-to-hand struggle followed, in which the loss of life on both sides was something enormous. The "Serapis" finally surrendered, but the "Richard" was so badly damaged that she sank the next day. The other frigate was captured by two smaller vessels, consorts of the "Bonhomme Richard," and this was the only part they took in the fight. No other engagement of any great consequence occurred on the ocean during the war.

But though the American navy during the Revolution was little more than a name (if it was even that), American privateersmen were something much more real, and the destruction inflicted by them upon British commerce was so very serious that it formed an important element in the war, and caused the English trading-classes to become very desirous of bringing the contest to a speedy end. Some of the privateersmen acted under the authority of Congress, and some under that of the separate States. The smaller war-ships built by Congress, which were not powerful enough to attack men-of-war, also employed themselves in worrying merchantmen of the enemy, and at one time for a brief period almost put an entire stop to England's foreign commerce.

PAUL JONES.

The British having gained control of Georgia, and kept it despite a vigorous attempt of Gen. Lincoln (the American commander in the South) to retake Savannah (Sept., 1779), they next turned their attention to South Carolina, and early in 1780 a large force sailed from New York under command of Clinton himself and, aided by troops from Georgia, laid siege to Charleston. Lincoln defended it to the best of his ability, but was at length compelled to surrender it (May, 1780), and with it his army of six thousand men. The whole State was then overrun as Georgia had been, and Clinton, satisfied with his work, returned to New York, leaving Cornwallis in command.

But though South Carolina and Georgia had been conquered, they did not lead their masters a very easy life. Gates, on whom the halo of Saratoga still rested, was first sent by Congress to take Lincoln's place, but his failure in his first Southern battle (Camden, N. C., August, 1780), notwithstanding knowing the country as only those born and brought up in it could, were able, from their hiding-places in forest and in swamp, to suddenly surprise the enemy with most unexpected attacks, to inflict the injury they had planned, and to depart as quickly as they had appeared.

While the attention of the people was fixed upon the South as the principal theatre of war, an event occurred in the North which produced a profound sensation throughout all the country and

PAUL JONES' SEA FIGHT.

his soldiers twice outnumbered the enemy, caused him quickly to give way to Gen. Nathanael Greene, who proved himself to be the one man for the work. Cautious, brave and alert, he kept the enemy constantly busy in long pursuits and in numerous battles, in which he was almost uniformly beaten, but in which the British losses were so much heavier than his own that his defeats were almost as valuable as victories would have been. He was ably seconded by Marion, Sumter, Morgan and other brilliant Southern cavalry officers, who, which might have been disastrous to the American cause. This was the treason of Benedict Arnold.

When the British left Philadelphia Arnold was given charge of the city, and there, tempted to spend more than he could afford, he used public money for his own purposes. For this, at the direction of Congress, he was reprimanded by Washington. Smarting with mortification and burning with revenge, he yet concealed his real purposes and after a time applied for the command of West Point. This was granted by Washington, who still had confidence in him on account of his earlier services in the war. No sooner had he reached his new post than he wrote to Clinton at New York, offering to turn the place over to the English for a sum of money and the position of brigadier-general in the British army. The offer was accepted and a young English officer, Major André, was sent to West Point to complete the arrangements. On his way back to New York he was taken prisoner near Tarrytown by three militiamen, who, on searching him, discovered plans of the fortifications at West Point hidden in his boots. Unfortunately, the officer in whose custody he was placed gave him an opportunity to write to Arnold, who, thus warned, escaped into the British lines before he could be captured. As André had been taken in disguise within the American lines, Washington reluctantly felt that there was no choice but to have him hung as a spy that others might be warned by his fate, and this was done (Oct., 1780), though the sympathy with him was almost universal.

BENEDICT ARNOLD.

MAJOR ANDRÉ.

CHAPTER XIII.

THE SURRENDER OF CORNWALLIS AND THE CLOSE OF THE WAR.

CLINTON was as desirous of subduing Virginia as he had been of overcoming Georgia and South Carolina, and the first task set Arnold on his receiving the reward of his villainy, was to lead an expedition from New York to the "Old Dominion" (January, 1781). Lafayette was sent by Washington to stop him, but could do nothing, as the French ships which were to help him were driven off by English men-of-war, so that Arnold plundered the State at will. Cornwallis, who in the course of his struggle with Greene had shifted his ground from Charleston to Wilmington (in North Carolina), determined to join the British forces in Virginia and try to complete its conquest. This he did, and stationed himself at Yorktown, which from its position on a peninsula he thought could be easily defended, and which also could readily be reached by British vessels. His combined army numbered eight thousand men, fully double as many as Lafayette's.

Cornwallis had scarcely got settled at Yorktown when Washington, still at Peekskill, received word that a large French force was on its way to the Chesapeake to cut off the British in Virginia from any assistance from the North. This was the chance for which he had been waiting, and his plans were quickly formed. Concealing his purpose from every one, he made a great show of preparation about New York to lead Clinton into thinking that that city was to be attacked, and under cover of the confusion began a rapid march to the South, hoping to arrive at Yorktown and capture Cornwallis before the British in New York could send relief to their countrymen.

His plan was successful. Clinton did not discover Washington's departure for several days, and when he learned the object of the movement and sent a British fleet to the aid of Cornwallis it was too late. The French had arrived at the Chesapeake and prevented the English from landing.

Before the arrival of Washington, Lafayette had

been reinforced with soldiers from the French fleet, and Washington also had with him a large body of soldiers which General De Rochambeau had brought over from France during the summer. Altogether there were sixteen thousand men who on the 30th of September, 1781, began the siege of Yorktown, a force amply large to shut the British completely off on the land side, while the French fleet under Admiral De Grasse as securely closed them in from the ocean.

Cornwallis was fairly trapped, and knew it. For three weeks he fought desperately to escape, but the line around him was too strong, and at last he had to give in, and on October 19, 1781, he laid down his arms and surrendered his army of eight thousand men to Washington. Had he held out a few days longer he might have been relieved, for an expedition of seven thousand men was on its way to him from New York, but this sailed back on learning his fate.

This ended the Revolution, for though no treaty was signed till two years afterwards, there were no more battles fought, and both sides, tired of the struggle, were quite content to cease all warfare while the two countries were settling upon the terms of peace. As finally agreed upon, the treaty placed the boundaries of the United States at Canada on the north, the Mississippi River on the west, and Florida on the south, and by it Great Britain fully recognized the independence of the country. Without waiting for its formal signing, the British gave up Savannah and Charleston in July and December, 1782, retaining possession only of New York and a few unimportant forts in the Northwest. New York remained in their hands a year longer, until news was received that the treaty had been ratified, and then that city also passed again to the control of the Americans—the last British soldier leaving it on November 25, 1783, a day whose anniversary is still observed in New York as "Evacuation Day."

CORNWALLIS.

THE SURRENDER OF CORNWALLIS AT YORKTOWN.

CHAPTER XIV.

FRAMING THE CONSTITUTION.

THE war was over, the army was disbanded, the Tories had left the country with their friends the British, and Washington had given back to Congress the commission of Commander-in-Chief which he had received from Congress. Peace had come, a peace which brought with it all that the country for nearly ten years had been striving for, absolute freedom and the right of self-government.

But it had also brought some other things with it: among them great discontent among the officers and men, who after enduring the most cruel sufferings and privations in the war received for their pay at its close only empty promises from Congress; paper money, which Congress had no means of redeeming and which soon became utterly worthless; and a weak general government which had very little authority and no power to enforce what little it had.

At the beginning of the war when the colonies became States they all adopted constitutions and formed governments which served excellently for their own separate needs. But they did nothing of the kind for the country at large. All that they did was to send delegates to the Continental Congress without giving them any real power to make laws or to tax the people. When Congress required money it was obliged to ask the States for it, and they gave it or not as they saw fit. In the early days of the conflict when there was great fear of England, the States were willing to do, and did do, pretty much everything requested of them, but after Burgoyne's surrender, when their confidence in themselves grew stronger, Congress had great difficulty in obtaining from them even a small part of what was actually needed to carry on the war, and at times the supply of food and clothing furnished the troops was so scanty that the soldiers rose in open rebellion, and Washington had the utmost trouble in pacifying them.

What had been bad during the Revolution grew much worse in the peace that followed, and soon there was the utmost disorder throughout the whole country. The States quarrelled among themselves about their boundaries; the larger ones passed laws which pressed heavily upon the smaller ones; the wishes and advice of Congress were disregarded more and more, so that it soon became the laughing-stock of the people. As a consequence of this condition of affairs there was distress everywhere, and for a time it looked as though the freedom which had been so dearly bought would prove a curse instead of a blessing.

This could not go on. The leading men saw that, if the country was to prosper and the newly won independence be of any benefit, the States must be united under some form of general government that had power both to make laws and to enforce them, a government that the people would respect because they would be compelled to obey it. A call was therefore issued for a convention of delegates from all the States to draw up a plan for the remedy of the evils under which the country was suffering.

In May, 1787, this Federal Convention met at Philadelphia, Rhode Island alone refusing to be represented. The States sent their ablest men, many of them young in years, but with unusual experience in public affairs gained during the Revolutionary War and the troubles which led to it. Washington was chosen its president. No one was admitted to its meetings but the delegates, and they pledged themselves to say nothing of its proceedings until its work was completed and published to the whole country.

Four months were spent by the Convention in settling upon a form of union that would suit all. Many times it seemed as if the delegates would be unable to agree and would have to give up the attempt and return to their homes. Most of the difficulty was with the smaller States, who were afraid that the larger States, on account of greater population and wealth, would have more power and influence than they, and that they would suffer in consequence. This fear was finally removed by providing that in the Senate every State should have an equal vote, and that the Senate's consent should be necessary for the passage of any law. The desire of the South to continue the slave trade was granted for twenty years on condition that after 1808 it was to cease forever. Other disagreements were arranged more or less readily by concessions on both sides and at last the Constitution as we now have it (without the Amendments) was perfected and submitted to the people for their approval.

The new Constitution proposed to replace the

former Confederation (as it had been called) with a government that could act and that could make its acts felt. The old government by Continental Congress had power only to recommend measures to the States. The new government was itself to have the power to make laws and to see that the laws which it made were duly carried into effect. It was to comprise three branches: a Congress to make laws, a President to enforce them, and courts of judges to explain them and to decide all questions that might arise under them. To accomplish this certain rights and privileges which they had previously possessed were taken away from the States and given to the new government. All their other powers the States were permitted to retain.

Its adoption by two-thirds of the States was necessary before it could go into operation, and nearly a year passed before this was secured, during which time it was eagerly debated throughout the length and breadth of the land. There was some opposition to it, chiefly on account of the powers of which it deprived the separate States, but the vast body of the people and nearly all of their leaders strongly favored it. New Hampshire was the ninth State to ratify it, and, as this completed the necessary number, arrangements were at once made to carry out its provisions by choosing a President and Vice-President and electing Members of Congress, and March 4, 1789, was set as the date for the beginning of the new government. Before that day arrived Virginia and New York had also adopted the Constitution, so that out of the thirteen States all but two took part in the first election, and these two were North Carolina and Rhode Island.

CHAPTER XV.

FORMATION OF THE NEW GOVERNMENT UNDER WASHINGTON.

THERE was but one voice as to who should be the first President of the young republic and that voice was for George Washington, the only President of the United States who has ever been chosen by a unanimous vote. Communication between the States was not as rapid at that time as it is in these days of railroad and telegraph, so that there was some delay in learning the results of the election, and it was not until April 30, 1789, that the inauguration of Washington took place, with great pomp and ceremony, in the city of New York. The spot in Wall Street where he took the oath of office is now marked by his statue.

WASHINGTON MADE PRESIDENT.

Washington immediately called to his assistance in conducting the government Thomas Jefferson, whom he appointed to be Secretary of State; Alexander Hamilton, whom he made Secretary of the Treasury; Gen. Knox, who became Secretary of War, and Edmund Randolph, as Attorney-General. These officers were to be the confidential advisers of the President and formed his Cabinet. Their positions were created by the new Congress, which was already in session when Washington began his administration. A few years later (1798) the Navy Department, which at first formed part of the War Department, was made a separate branch of the government and its Secretary added to the Cabinet. The Post-Office and In-

FORMATION OF THE NEW GOVERNMENT UNDER WASHINGTON. 65

INSTALLATION OF WASHINGTON.

terior Departments were not created until 1829 and 1849 respectively, and the Department of Agriculture not until 1889. The most important of Washington's other appointments was that of John Jay as Chief Justice of the Supreme Court.

The wisdom of Washington's choice of his advisers soon showed itself in the organization of the machinery of government, whose running from the first was as smooth as though it had long been in operation. Under advice from the Cabinet, Congress passed the necessary laws to give full effect to the Constitution, and so great a care was taken to start everything in the right way that during the hundred years that have since passed few changes have been made in the methods then adopted excepting such as were required by the growing size of the public business. The strong and firm hand of the government quickly restored order to the disturbed country and afforded an opportunity for laying the foundations of the wonderful prosperity that has since marked the progress of the nation. The invention of the cotton-gin by Whitney in 1793 became a great source of wealth to the country, as it enabled one person to separate the seeds from a thousand pounds of cotton in the same time that it had previously taken him to clean six pounds. Unfortunately it also caused an increased demand for slave labor, and made it less probable that slavery would die out in the South, as it was already doing in the North. The boundary disputes had been partly settled shortly before Washington became President, and soon were all arranged, the States giving up the western lands they had claimed to the new government, which thus became possessed of a large and rich tract of territory out of which some of the richest and most populous States have since been formed.

One of the earliest acts of Congress was to choose a capital for the United States, and a site was accordingly selected on the banks of the Potomac, to which it was decided that the government should be removed in 1800. Until then it was to meet at Philadelphia. A system of taxation to provide for the public expenses and for the payment of the debt incurred during the Revolution was prepared by Hamilton and adopted, and twelve amendments to the Constitution were proposed by which the rights of the States were more expressly guarded than in the Constitution itself. Ten of these amendments were ratified by the people, and in 1791 became part of the Constitution.

In the meantime North Carolina (in 1789) and Rhode Island (in 1790) had given their assent to the new form of government, and the thirteen States that had struggled together through the war were

ELI WHITNEY.

DANIEL BOONE.

once more united. Other States soon began to ask admittance to the Union, and the first to be received was Vermont. She originally had been part of the grant made by King Charles to the Duke of York, but was claimed also by New Hampshire. While New York was disputing this claim and the two colonies were quarrelling over her, the "Green Mountain boys" (Vermont is the French for "green mountain") set up a government for themselves which they kept up during the Revolution (in which they did good service) and until her entrance into the sisterhood of States in 1791. Kentucky followed the next year. She had been part of Virginia, and her settlement was begun in 1769 by Daniel Boone, one of the boldest and bravest frontiersmen in American history. The Indians opposed its colonization very stubbornly, and the whites had to fight their way for possession foot by foot. She had Virginia's full consent in seeking and obtaining the privileges of statehood. The third State to be admitted during Washington's presidency was Tennessee. Until 1784 she was part of North Carolina, but in that year she revolted and tried to form an independent government under the name of Franklin. In this she failed, and in 1790 was given by North Carolina to the United States. She was known as the Southwest Territory from that date until 1796, when under her present name she became the sixteenth State. Both Kentucky and Tennessee are the Indian names of rivers that flow through the two States.

A WESTERN HOMESTEAD.

MOUNT VERNON.

The Constitution placed the terms of President and Vice-President at four years, but the sentiment in favor of Washington's re-election in 1792 was as strong as it had been when he was first chosen in 1788. When his second term expired in 1797 the people would gladly have elected him for a third time had he not positively refused to accept the office again. Before retiring to his home at Mount Vernon (in Virginia) he issued a Farewell Address, intended not only for the Americans of that day, but for those that came after them as well, in which he counselled his countrymen how they could best preserve the freedom they had gained. This paper ranks with the Declaration of Independence and the Constitution of the United States as one of our three priceless charters of liberty. The love and veneration of the whole country accompanied Washington in his retirement, and when two years later, in his sixty-eighth year, he died (Dec. 14, 1799), his loss was mourned by the entire nation as one man. The greatest of all Americans, no one before his time nor since it has for one moment rivalled the affection which he holds in the hearts of the people to whom he gave independence.

CHAPTER XVI.

THE BEGINNING OF PARTY POLITICS.

ALEXANDER HAMILTON.

THE second President of the United States was not elected with the unanimity with which the first had been chosen; on the contrary he met with considerable opposition. For when the time came (1796) to select a successor to Washington it found the people divided into two political parties, each of which had a candidate in the field whom it was urging for the presidency.

The first of these parties, called the Federalist, was the party which had done most to secure the adoption of the Constitution, which had organized the new government, and which carried it through the first eight years of its existence. Its two most eminent leaders were John Adams and Alexander Hamilton. Washington's sympathies were really with it, though he took no side and was strictly impartial in conducting his administration.

With a vivid recollection of the discomforts and evils caused by the weak government of the Continental Congress and of the Confederation, the Federalists held that the only safety for the people, the only way in which they could prosper, was in a strong central government with the most ample powers for ruling the country. Otherwise, they said, the jealousies and dissensions among the States would forever hinder the progress of the nation and finally bring it to ruin.

Opposed to the Federalists were the Republicans, led by Thomas Jefferson. They too looked to the experience of the past to guide them in the present, but it was in the troubles before the Revolution that they found their lesson. Appealing to the memory

JOHN ADAMS.

of men to recall how the liberties of the colonies had once suffered under the strong arm of a great power, they besought their fellow-citizens not to again endanger them by transferring to this new general government any of the rights belonging to the States excepting those absolutely necessary to give effect to the Constitution. They feared that the new government might become so strong as to crush the States, and they felt that each State best knew the needs of its own people and could best advance their interests. In brief, the difference between the two parties was this: the Federalists would strengthen the general government at the expense, if needful, of the States: while the Republicans would maintain State rights even if it left the general government weak. It should be noted that the Republicans of that day were an entirely distinct party from the Republicans of the present time.

Adams and Jefferson were the candidates of their parties, and after a sharp contest the former won, the latter becoming Vice-President. The new President was well experienced in public affairs, having

AARON BURR.

THE CAPITOL AT WASHINGTON.

THE BEGINNING OF PARTY POLITICS.

been Vice-President during both of Washington's terms and prior to that United States Minister to England, being, in fact, the first representative sent to Great Britain by this country after its independence was acknowledged. A native of Massachusetts, he was foremost among her sons in defending her rights during the struggle which preceded the Revolution, and was equally zealous while the war lasted in advocating the cause of the young republic in Europe. On the conclusion of the conflict he was one of those appointed to draw up and sign in behalf of the United States the treaty of peace with Great Britain.

The administration of Adams cannot be said to have been a remarkably successful one for the country, and it proved a fatal one to his party.

MAIN ENTRANCE TO THE WHITE HOUSE.

THE WHITE HOUSE, WASHINGTON.

Trouble with France, then in a very unsettled condition resulting from the French Revolution, occupied most of its attention and nearly led to war. Indeed there was some actual fighting on the sea, but nothing of any importance excepting the defeat and capture of "L'Insurgente" by the "Constellation" under Commodore Truxton off the West Indies (1799). Congress had made preparations for war and was about to declare it when a change in the French government by which Napoleon Bonaparte became its head removed the difficulties between the two nations and assured peace between them once more.

It was not the threatened war with France which wrecked the Federalists. That was popular. But it was the passage of two laws by their party in Congress during the excitement of the period that cost them the confidence of the people; and these were the Alien and Sedition Laws, permitting the arrest of any foreigner (alien) regarded as dangerous and of any person who spoke evil of the government. These were both intended to strengthen the hands of the President and of the executive government and were in accord with the policy of the Federalists, but they were bitterly opposed by the Republicans, who declared that no man ought to be imprisoned unless convicted by a jury of some crime, and that it was one of the rights of the citizen to criticise the government, for without such criticism true freedom could not exist. In this a majority of the people agreed with them, and at the election in 1800 Adams was defeated and Jefferson was chosen President in his stead. Jefferson did not obtain the coveted prize, however, until after a rather peculiar contest with his political friend, Aaron Burr, the candidate of the

SOUTH FRONT OF THE WHITE HOUSE.

Republicans for Vice-President, which showed a curious defect in the Constitution.

The presidential electors, at that time, in choosing the President and Vice-President simply voted for two men without specifying on their ballots which office each was to hold, and the one who received the most votes became President and he who had the next highest number became Vice-President. By this method, the framers of the Constitution thought, the best man would be selected President and the next best Vice-President. It does not seem to have oc-

PENSION OFFICE.

curred to them that the electors might be divided into political parties, the members of each casting ballots all having on them the same two names. But this was what did happen in 1800. All the Republicans voted for both Jefferson and Burr, who thus had an equal number of votes.

STATE, NAVY AND WAR DEPARTMENT BUILDING.

TREASURY BUILDING.

Every one knew, of course, which the electors meant should be President and which Vice-President, but there was nothing on the ballots to indicate it. The decision between the two thereupon fell to the House of Representatives (or lower branch of Congress), which, after some little delay and trouble caused by the friends of Burr, gave the presidency, as it was intended to go, to Jefferson. Before another election came round an amendment to the Constitution was adopted which prevented the recurrence of such a difficulty by directing the electors to vote for the two offices separately.

The year which witnessed the defeat of Adams and the expulsion from power of the Federalists saw also the removal of the seat of government from Philadelphia to the banks of the Potomac. The new city which the First Congress, ten years before, had ordered should be laid out as a permanent home for the federal government, and which in honor of the Father of his Country had been named Washington, was then a city only in name; in appearance it was more like a small country village, with muddy and unpaved streets, mean-looking houses and small population. It is only within a short number of years that the stately buildings, which now render it one of the most beautiful of American cities, have been erected and that it has assumed something of the dignity of a national capital.

CHAPTER XVII.

THE ADMINISTRATION OF JEFFERSON.

As Governor of Virginia, Minister to France, Secretary of State under Washington and Vice-President under Adams, Thomas Jefferson had already shown himself to be one of the wisest statesmen of his time before he was called to the high office of President. The Declaration of Independence was the work of his hand, the Republican (soon to be known as the Democratic) party the fruit of his political teachings. Few men have been able to impress their beliefs more durably on the history and laws of their country than did the third President of the United States.

He served for two terms, taking office in 1801 and leaving it in 1809. During these eight years the number of States was increased by one and the area of the United States was more than doubled. The new State was Ohio, and it had been part of that large western tract of land about which the older States had once quarrelled and which fifteen years or more before they had given to the general government. In accepting the gift of this Northwest Territory (as it was called) the Congress of the Confederation had, by what is known as the Ordinance of 1787, thrown it open to general settlement and had agreed that as the population in it increased five States should in turn be formed from it and admitted to the Union. The Ordinance also prohibited slavery from forever being tolerated within the borders of this Territory, and it guaranteed to all who should settle in it equal political rights and perfect religious freedom. This agreement or Ordinance was afterwards confirmed by the new government formed under the Constitution.

THOMAS JEFFERSON.

The first settlement by Americans in Ohio was at Marietta in 1788, followed by another in the same year at Losantiville, now Cincinnati. The Indians at once opened war upon the immigrants and for a time held them in check, but in 1794 General Wayne States which thus far had entered the Union, an equal number were free (Vermont and Ohio) and an equal number were slave (Kentucky and Tennessee).

Ohio was admitted in 1802. In the following year the territory of Louisiana, which shortly before had been sold by Spain to France, was bought by the United States from Napoleon Bonaparte for fifteen millions of dollars. This territory embraced far more than the present State of that name, and added over a million square miles to the eight hundred thousand which had previously comprised the area of the country. The next year (1804) the foundation was laid for still another enlargement of the boundaries of the United States by an exploring

ANTHONY WAYNE.

was sent by President Washington to Ohio, and he defeated the Indians so completely that they gave up the State to the whites. Wayne was one of the heroes of the Revolution, where for his great daring he was nicknamed "Mad Anthony." Like Kentucky and Tennessee, Ohio took its name from that

NAPOLEON BONAPARTE.

expedition under Lewis and Clarke through Oregon, Idaho and Washington (State), a region hitherto unvisited by Americans. Great Britain afterwards disputed the claim which this exploration gave us to that part of America, and the question of ownership remained unsettled for over forty years.

But the occurrence of this period which is of the most importance, by the side of which the purchase of Louisiana and the exploration of the Oregon country seem of trifling value, was the invention by Robert Fulton of the steamboat. Since Watt had invented the steam-engine forty years before, the effort had repeatedly been made to apply it to vessels, but without much success until Fulton's boat, the

ROBERT FULTON.

given by the Indians to its principal river, but unlike those two States its soil (as provided in the Ordinance of 1787) was free. Of the four new

"Clermont," made the journey to Albany, driven by steam, in 1807. Steamships were soon seen on the waters of all the inhabited parts of the country, and were of the greatest possible service in developing and building up the districts which as yet had not been settled.

When Jefferson was re-elected President in 1804, Burr, who had lost much of his popularity, was not continued as Vice-President. Disappointed at his political failure, he organized an expedition in 1807 to go to the southwest, and there to set up a government of his own separate from the United States. Before he could carry out his plans he was arrested and tried for treason, but as he had not actually borne arms against the United States he could not be convicted.

FULTON'S STEAMBOAT.

This, together with his having killed Hamilton in a duel, which he had forced upon Hamilton (1804), filled the measure of his public disgrace and the rest of his life was passed in the closest retirement. Hamilton, strong partisan as he was, had been especially esteemed by the people, and his early death in such a manner gave the country a shock that soon put an end to the practice of duelling.

Fulton's invention was not used in sending ships across the Atlantic for a number of years after it had been successfully applied to river boats. But our foreign commerce had not waited for the completion of that invention to become an important element in our prosperity. Securing a good start under Washington, it had grown very rapidly until under Jefferson American vessels were carrying a large part of the freight

STEPHEN DECATUR.

74   HISTORY OF THE UNITED STATES.

of the world. This good fortune was mainly due to the wars in which nearly all of Europe was at the time engaged, and which made the ships of a neutral like ourselves the safest for the transportation of goods.

An annoying hindrance to this commerce had for a long time existed in the tribute which the Barbary States on the northern shores of Africa compelled Christian nations to pay to prevent their ships from being captured and their sailors from being sold into slavery by these Mohammedan face of a constant fire from the enemy burned her. The damage done to her forts and shipping by frequent bombardments finally brought Tripoli to terms, and in 1805 she yielded and made peace with the United States. The example thus set by America in resisting the Mediterranean pirates was followed by other nations, and in the course of a few years a complete stop was put to their exactions.

But before Jefferson's presidency ended American commerce suffered from a much more serious inter-

DECATUR BURNING THE "PHILADELPHIA."

pirates. The United States, like the nations of Europe, submitted to this extortion until Tripoli (one of these Barbary States) in 1801 increased the amount of money demanded. This the United States refused to pay and sent her little navy to the Mediterranean to protect American ships. The "Philadelphia," one of her frigates, having stranded in the harbor of Tripoli, was captured (1803), but before the Mohammedans had any chance to make use of her, a boat-load of sailors, pluckily led by Lieutenant Decatur, ran into the harbor, and in ference than from the Barbary tax. This was from the blockades which England and France declared against the ports of each other and of their allies. Not content with these blockades, Great Britain went further, and in 1807 issued Orders in Council forbidding any American ship from entering any European harbor excepting her own and those of her friend, Sweden. Bonaparte replied with his Milan Decree directing that every American vessel which entered a British port should, if captured by the French, be sold.

Between these two cross-fires our foreign trade was soon in a sorry plight. The people felt these acts to be intolerable, but were reluctant to go to war, as the weakness of the American navy offered but a poor chance of any redress from fighting. Moreover the Republicans were more desirous of paying off the debt already incurred than of burdening the country with a new one, as a war would do. It was therefore decided to stop all trade for a time with Europe in the hope that the injury thus inflicted upon foreign commerce would bring the two countries to terms. Accordingly in 1807 Congress passed the Embargo Act, prohibiting any vessel from leaving the United States for any European port.

Instead of helping matters this only made them worse. Great Britain profited by it in getting back some of the carrying trade she had previously lost, and New England, whose foreign business was large, suffered severely from the paralysis caused it by this step. All of the country was affected more or less from the measure, and in 1809 it was found necessary to replace the Embargo Act by the Non-Intercourse Act, which, while still forbidding trade with France and England, permitted it with other countries. This made the situation a little better, but not a great deal, and the feeling became very bitter against France and Great Britain, particularly against the latter, as she had been the more hostile of the two.

CHAPTER XVIII.

THE WAR OF 1812.

Though the troubles with France and England had lost to the Republicans some of their popularity with the people, they yet succeeded in electing one of their number President when Jefferson's second term expired in 1809. This was James Madison, also a Virginian, and, like his predecessors, of public experience derived from services in his State legislature, the Constitutional Convention and Congress. He had been Secretary of State under Jefferson.

The foreign difficulties under Madison did not improve; they rather grew worse. France, indeed, did agree to repeal her decrees if the Non-Intercourse Act was not applied against her, but England enforced the Orders in Council with greater vigor than ever, and stationed war ships along the American coast ready to pounce upon any vessel that ventured forth. What was particularly hateful to the Americans was the right claimed and continually exercised by her of stopping the ships of any nation upon the high seas and taking away any sailors whom the officer making the search chose to think had been born in Great Britain or Ireland. In this way many American citizens, both native and naturalized, were forced into the British navy and compelled to serve against their own country. Not content with these injuries, the British attempted also to inflict one of a different kind by aiding some Indians under Tecumseh in an attack upon the whites in the Northwest. General W. H. Harrison defeated these Indians (1811) at Tippecanoe, and Tecumseh with his men afterwards entered the British army.

At length the patience of the Americans became exhausted, and on June 18, 1812, Congress, after making what preparations it could, formally declared war against Great Britain. The government had

JAMES MADISON.

HISTORY OF THE UNITED STATES.

TECUMSEH.

but little money at its command and these preparations were not very formidable. The navy consisted of only twelve vessels, and the army was an undisciplined body of troops officered by Revolutionary soldiers, now too old to be really efficient, or by politicians ignorant of the first principles of military science. Among the Federalists and throughout New England the war was not regarded with much favor, but the Republicans strongly supported it, and they formed a decided majority of the people.

Most of the honors in the naval part of the conflict fell to the Americans. On the land they were more evenly divided. The naval results were a surprise to the United States as well as to England and to Europe generally, for hitherto the British had been considered almost invincible on the ocean even by a first-class power, which America at that time certainly was not. Out of the seventeen sea-fights which occurred during the two and a half years that the war lasted, the Americans won thirteen and lost four, and this surely was a creditable showing for a nation which at the beginning of the contest had only a handful of war ships to oppose to the thousand belonging to the enemy. The disparity between the sea forces of the two countries, however, did not long continue to be quite as great as this, for the United States soon very materially increased its navy by the purchase and building of more vessels.

The reason for this was very largely in the carelessness of the English commanders and in the vigilance of their opponents. The very success which Great Britain had so uniformly met with hitherto

THE "CHESAPEAKE" AND THE "SHANNON."

on the ocean made her now more lax, especially when she had a nation so much her inferior in power as the United States to contend against. The Americans, on the contrary, were all the more alert because they felt their weakness. Whatever they were to accomplish must be done by discipline and skill, for of strength they had but little as compared with that against them.

The first of these sea-victories was the capture of the "Alert" by the "Essex" commanded by Captain Porter, followed in a few days by the capture of the "Guerriere" by the "Constitution" under Captain Hull. This was in August, 1812. In the following October the "Frolic" was taken by the "Wasp" (Captain Jacob Jones), and the "Macedonian" by the "United States" (Captain Decatur). Still a fifth conquest was made the same year (December)—that of the "Java" by the "Constitution," now under command of Captain William Bainbridge. Against these five victories was one loss, the "Wasp," which was so badly injured in its fight with the "Frolic" that it fell an easy prey to the "Poictiers," a larger British vessel, which overtook and captured it with its prize a few hours afterwards.

During 1813 the American navy was not quite as successful as it had been in the preceding year, its defeats equalling in number its victories. Of its losses, that of the "Chesapeake" (June) was the most serious. The "Chesapeake" was commanded by Captain Lawrence, who earlier in the season (February), while in command of the "Hornet," had gained one of the two victories of the year by defeating and capturing the "Peacock." For this service he had been transferred to the larger ship, the "Chesapeake," but had scarcely assumed charge before he was engaged in battle with the "Shannon." Lawrence fought gallantly, but in this case British discipline was better than American and prevailed. Lawrence lost his life before the struggle was decided, so that he was spared the pain of defeat. His last words—" Don't give up the ship"—became for the rest of the war the battle-cry of the American sailor.

Of the other ocean reverses the capture of the "Essex" (March, 1814) was the most important. She had been cruising in the Pacific for about a year when she was attacked, while crippled from an accident, by the "Phœbe" and "Cherub," and after the fiercest fight of the war, during which more than half of her men were killed, she was forced to surrender. Another loss to the Americans occurred in the following January when the "President" was taken by a British fleet near Long Island.

But against these disasters was a long series of splendid successes: the "Peacock" over the "Epervier" (April, 1814); the "Wasp" over the "Reindeer" (June, 1814); the "Wasp" over the "Avon" (Sept., 1814); the "Constitution" over the "Cyane" and the "Levant" (Feb., 1815); the "Hornet" over the "Penguin" (March, 1815); and the "Peacock" over the "Nautilus" (June, 1815). The three captures (all under different commanders) made by the "Constitution" earned her the reputation of a lucky ship with her officers and men and they gave her the name of "Old Ironsides," by which she was known as long as she was kept afloat.

OLIVER HAZARD PERRY.

Not only on the ocean was the United States successful. Two of its greatest naval victories were won on the lakes. Captain Perry had command on Lake Erie, his fleet consisting of five small vessels and two larger ones, the "Lawrence" and the "Niagara," the former named after the hero of the "Chesapeake," whose dying words were inscribed on the flag flying from her mast. In September, 1813, Perry met the British fleet and engaged it in battle. He was in the "Lawrence," and against her the English at first directed the whole of their fire until she became hopelessly disabled. Quickly shifting himself to the "Niagara," Perry turned at once upon the British, exhausted from their attack on the "Lawrence," and breaking through their line poured upon them so heavy a fire in all directions that in a quarter of an hour the entire fleet surrendered. Perry used few words to announce his victory: "We have met the enemy and they are ours: two ships, two brigs, one schooner, and one sloop."

The victory on Lake Erie gave the American army an opportunity to invade Canada. Exactly a year later (Sept. 11, 1814) a similar success on Lake Champlain prevented an English army from invading New York by way of Canada. Commodore Macdonough was at the head of the American fleet on this lake which opposed the progress of the British, and the result of the battle was the capture of the four larger vessels of the enemy, the flight of the smaller ones and the retreat of the army. In neither of these lake engagements did the Americans have quite as many guns or men as the English. Indeed there were few naval battles in the war in which whatever advantage there might be in these respects did not rest with the British.

Turning now to land operations the picture is not as flattering to American pride, for there we did not have it nearly so much our own way as on the water. At the outset of the war several attempts were made to invade Canada, but they only resulted in the loss of Detroit (Aug., 1812), then the largest town on the northwestern frontier. General W. H. Harrison was then given command of the West and he tried many times to retake Detroit, but his troops at first were too raw to accomplish much. It was while he was striving to drive the enemy from Michigan that the battle of the Raisin River occurred (Jan., 1813), long remembered for the bloody massacre of the wounded by the Indians which followed it and which was inhumanly permitted by the British commander, General Proctor. The victory of Perry finally afforded Harrison the chance to enter Canada, where he defeated Proctor at the Thames River (Oct., 1813), killed Tecumseh and put an end to the war in that region. Detroit and other captured forts were easily retaken and Michigan passed back again to American control.

WINFIELD SCOTT.

In northern New York there was the same ill-success for the first year or two that there was in the West, and the same improvement in the latter part of the war. The most important engagement in this section of the country was the battle of Lundy's Lane (July, 1814), fought on the Canadian side of the Niagara River, which resulted in driving the British from the field, but also in weakening the Americans so seriously that they thought it prudent to themselves retire as well the next day. The improved discipline in this northern army was principally due to the efforts of Winfield Scott, one of the younger officers lately put in command, and who, with Ripley and Jacob Brown, led our soldiers in the battle of Lundy's Lane.

In the East the American cause suffered even more than in the West and North. The British vessels stationed along the Atlantic coast not only blockaded all the ports but they bombarded many towns and sent parties on shore who did much injury to public and private property. Lewes, Havre de Grace, Hampton and Stonington were among the places thus attacked, and New York only escaped through British fear of the torpedoes in the harbor. But the greatest disaster in this region, in fact of the war, was the burning of Washington. That city had been left entirely unprotected, and when an English army of five thousand men landed at Chesapeake Bay and marched to the seat of government (Aug., 1814) there were no soldiers there to defend it and the city was pillaged at will.

This work of destruction accomplished, the British turned to Baltimore, but here some preparations for defence had been made and the attack was determinedly resisted and finally repulsed.

The Indians on the frontier, who were generally hostile to the settlers, nearly everywhere seized the occasion of the outbreak of the war to attack the whites. Of these attacks by far the most serious was that made by the Creeks, the principal tribe in the Southwest Territory consisting of the present States of Alabama and Mississippi. In August, 1813, they surprised Fort Mims (near Mobile) and put to death nearly all of the five hundred men, women and children who had taken refuge there.

Such an act called for immediate vengeance. The Tennessee militia hastened to the field and under command of Andrew Jackson pursued the Indians, and at the battle of Tohopeka, on the Tallapoosa River (Alabama), overwhelmingly routed them, killing eight hundred of their number and

PACKENHAM LEADING THE ATTACK ON NEW ORLEANS.

compelling them to give up most of their land to the Americans (March, 1814). From this time the Creeks, who before had been a power in the Southwest, gave the settlers but little trouble.

The battle of Tohopeka, or Horseshoe Bend (as it is also called), made Jackson's reputation for leadership and the command in the Southwest was given to him. It was known that an army was on its way from England to attack New Orleans, and Jackson at once made the most energetic arrangements for its defence. Entrenchments were thrown up on marshy land a few miles below New Orleans and expert riflemen stationed behind them to prevent the enemy on landing from reaching the city.

In December, 1814, the British arrived. They comprised twelve thousand veteran troops led by Sir Edward Packenham, and opposed to them were six thousand Americans as inexperienced in war as were the minute-men at Lexington and Concord. The first week or two was spent in minor skirmishes, and then, on January 8, 1815, Packenham threw his entire army against Jackson's works. Profiting by the example of their fathers at Bunker Hill, the Americans held back their fire until the English were close at hand and then poured it upon them with such deadly effect that the whole line of the enemy broke and fled, leaving their commander and over twenty-five hundred of their number dead behind them, while of Jackson's men but seven were killed and thirteen wounded.

The battle of New Orleans was a more gratifying close to the war than Hull's surrender of Detroit had been a beginning of it. Before this last battle was fought peace had been concluded by American and British representatives at the Belgian city of Ghent (Dec. 24, 1814), but the news of it did not reach this country until after Jackson's victory. It is curious that the very things which caused the two countries to begin the war were neither of them mentioned in the treaty of peace. The reason for their omission is that they had ceased to be of importance. England and France were no longer at war and hence there was no occasion for the former to enforce her Orders in Council. As to the British claim to the right of search and imprisonment of seamen, the United States no longer feared she would attempt to exercise it, as the American navy had shown itself fully able to protect our commerce on the ocean.

Tidings of peace were never more gladly received than was the news of the treaty of Ghent. Though it left matters very much as they were before, it was everywhere hailed with delight and celebrated by the ringing of bells and firing of cannon. For by the close of the war business of all kinds was nearly at a standstill. The people had become too poor to buy anything but the barest necessities of life, and sometimes they could hardly buy those. Money was scarce, creditors could not collect their debts, farmers could not sell their crops. New England suffered especially from the stoppage put to her commerce by the war. From the first she had opposed it, and the many land reverses met with by the Americans during its progress did not tend to decrease her opposition. This opposition grew still stronger after the burning of Washington, and in the latter part of 1814 a secret convention of New England Federalists was held at Hartford, to take steps, the Republicans said, to withdraw from the Union. There is no proof to support this charge, for all the convention did was to draw up a report on the condition of the country, suggest that New England be allowed to defend herself against the English without waiting for Federal aid and propose some changes in the Constitution. Peace so quickly followed the meetings of the convention that nothing came of its recommendations.

BRIDGE OVER THE MISSISSIPPI RIVER AT ST. LOUIS.

CHAPTER XIX.

THE ERA OF GOOD FEELING AND THE MISSOURI COMPROMISE.

THE close of the war opened again the ocean roads for merchant ships to Europe, and with the resumption of foreign commerce came a revival of business throughout the land. The country was growing. The war itself had stimulated the settlement of western New York, which previously had been a rarely visited wilderness. Steamboats were carrying emigrants to the West and Jackson's crushing defeat of the Creeks had removed all fear of the Indians in Alabama and Mississippi and thrown them open to white colonists. New States were also coming into the Union. In 1812 Louisiana was separated from the rest of the territory bought from France and given statehood, followed four years later (1816) by Indiana, formed, as Ohio had been, from the Northwest Territory. Slavery was already in existence in Louisiana before it became a State, while the Ordinance of 1787 insured free soil in Indiana and the rest of the Northwest Territory. The admission of these two States therefore did not affect the balance of power between the slaveholding and non-slaveholding States.

The opposition of the Federalists to the war and particularly their calling the Hartford Convention destroyed what little influence they still had. They had been unable to prevent the re-election of Madison in 1812; they were able to do yet less in 1816 when Madison's successor was to be chosen. Out of two hundred and twenty-one electoral votes cast, the Republican candidate, Monroe, received all but thirty-four. This ended the Federalist party. It now completely disappeared from politics and at no future election did it make even a nomination for office. After a few years a new party was formed, called the Whig, and this was joined by many of those who were formerly Federalists. But in the meantime there was little or no organized opposition to the Republicans, who in consequence were able to conduct the government pretty much as they liked.

James Monroe, the fifth President of the United States and the fourth furnished by Virginia, had had perhaps even a wider experience in public office than any of the Presidents before him. He had served as captain in the Revolution, as member of the Continental Congress, and (on the adoption of the Constitution) as United States Senator. Then he became Minister in succession to France, England and Spain, and afterwards Governor of Virginia and (under Madison) Secretary of State. He held the presidency for eight years, only one electoral vote being cast against him at the end of his first term in 1820, and that was thrown simply that no one should share with Washington the honor of a unanimous election.

The administration of Monroe was the "era of

JAMES MONROE.

good feeling." Parties and politics for the time were over. The country was at peace and was prosperous, and its increasing population was forming settlements in every direction and rapidly developing its marvellous resources. The three millions of people contained in the United States at the end of the War for Independence had by 1820 become over nine and a half millions, and these figures were constantly enlarging by a vast emigration from Europe which spread itself over the country, clearing away forests, building villages and towns, and turning the wilderness into a garden.

HISTORY OF THE UNITED STATES.

Railroads were as yet unknown. The only means of travel were by boat or carriage. The importance therefore of good roads and waterways was manifest. Recognizing this, Congress and the various

DE WITT CLINTON.

States, in order to aid in the development of the country, began at this time to build a better system of roads and canals than any that had hitherto existed. Of these by far the most extensive and important was the Erie Canal, constructed by the State of New York, and which, by connecting Lake Erie at Buffalo with the Hudson at Albany, afforded a new outlet from the Great Lakes to the Atlantic and made travel and traffic between New York and what was then the extreme West immensely easier. Eight years were occupied in its building (1817-1825), and the credit of the enterprise is due to the untiring efforts of Governor De Witt Clinton, but for whom it never would have been begun or pushed to a conclusion. It is undoubtedly to the Erie Canal that New York owes the commercial supremacy she has so long enjoyed and which has made her to-day the largest and wealthiest of the States.

Once before had the United States added to its territory. Now it did so again by buying (1821), for five millions of dollars, Florida from Spain, to whom it had been given by England at the close of the Revolution. This purchase was rendered necessary, or at least desirable, by the trouble which both the Indians and Spanish settlers in Florida continually gave to the neighboring Americans in Georgia and Alabama, and which could not readily be checked until our government obtained control of the territory.

Not only was the area of the United States enlarged during this period, but the number of States was increased and five more stars added to the American flag. The first to be admitted was Mississippi (1817), originally claimed by Georgia, but given up in 1802 to Congress. Next followed Illinois (in 1818), the third State taken from the Northwest Territory. Alabama, which like Mississippi had once belonged to Georgia, came in 1819, and a year later Maine was divided off from Massachusetts and made a State by itself. The last of these five was Missouri, admitted in 1821. The names of all these States, excepting Maine, were taken from the Indians, Illinois being the name of a tribe and the

THE FIRST BOAT THROUGH THE CANAL TO THE SEA.

others the names of rivers. Maine received its name from the French possessions of Henrietta Maria, wife of Charles the First, during whose reign it was first settled.

THE ERA OF GOOD FEELING AND THE MISSOURI COMPROMISE. 83

Missouri was part of the Territory of Missouri, the name given to the rest of the French purchase when Louisiana was cut off from it and made a State in 1812. Its admission raised the slavery question and marks the beginning of the anti-slavery struggle, which was not brought to a final close till nearly half a century later. Though negroes were at first held in bondage in all of the original thirteen colonies, they were never as numerous in the North as in the South, and the idea of slavery was never as well liked in the one region as in the other. Before the end of the last century it had nearly died out in the North and public sentiment there was becoming decidedly averse to it, while in the South, on the other hand, it was constantly increasing as negro labor became more profitable in the production of cotton, rice and tobacco. But however much the North might be opposed to the principle of slavery there was no thought at first of attempting to abolish it in the Southern States where it already existed. There was, however, a strong feeling against its extension to new parts of the country, and it was this feeling which had secured (by the Ordinance of 1787) its prohibition from the Northwest Territory.

Of the ten States admitted into the Union after the adoption of the Constitution, and up to the time that Missouri came in, five (Vermont, Ohio, Indiana, Illinois and Maine) had been free and five (Kentucky, Tennessee, Louisiana, Alabama and Mississippi) slave. In the latter five slavery had been introduced before they passed under control of the national government either by gift from the older States or (as in the case of Louisiana) by purchase. There was therefore but little objection to their admission as slave States. The case of Missouri was thought to be different. In position she was nearer to the Northern States than to the Southern ones, and her interests, the North claimed, would lie more with the former than with the latter, and like them, therefore, she should be free. She was west of the Mississippi, and the North held that the founders of the government had never intended that slavery should extend beyond that river. When bought from France there had been scarcely any settlement within her boundaries, so that her soil was then virtually free, and only as a free State were the opponents of slavery willing she should enter the Union. But during her territorial days many slave-owners had moved into Missouri and they had become a majority of her population. They naturally wished to retain their slave property, and in this they were supported by the other Southern States, who argued that the Constitution had left the matter to the States, and that if Missouri chose to permit slavery she was entitled to do so. Congress debated the question long and earnestly, public feeling in both sections of the country becoming thoroughly roused and excited.

ERIE CANAL, NEW YORK STATE.

Finally, after a discussion which lasted two years, the dispute was arranged by admitting Missouri as a slave State on condition that all other territories and future States north of her southern boundary should be free. It was hoped at the time that this "Missouri Compromise," as it was called, would end forever the slavery contest, but as will be seen later on it only postponed the day of settlement.

Monroe's administration saw also the opening of another great public question which, unlike that of slavery, has not yet reached a final settlement. This was the tariff question. Many manufactories had been established in this country since the Revolutionary times, but their owners found it difficult to compete with foreign (especially English) goods, which were offered for sale in the American markets more cheaply than they could be profitably made for here. At the request of American manufacturers, Congress in 1824 increased the taxes (or duties) on goods imported into this country so as to raise the price at which they must be sold, and thus protect home wares. This protective policy was (and is) opposed by those who believe that the government ought not to do anything to restrict trade, that every one should have the right to buy where he can buy at the least cost, and that a high tariff compels the many to support the few. From that time to the present this question of free trade or protection has often come up for discussion and action, and the people have sometimes inclined to one side and sometimes to the other, but they have never yet spoken so decisively for either policy as to cause its opponents to abandon the contest.

The "Monroe Doctrine," which has ever since been our great guide in determining the relations we should hold with foreign countries, also originated in this period. It was set forth in a message sent to Congress by the President in the year preceding the adoption of the protective tariff, and declared that while the United States would take no part in any quarrel or war between the nations of Europe or disturb any colony already established in this country, we would not permit any European interference with the affairs of this continent, any attempt to plant new colonies or to subject any independent state to the condition of a colony in either North or South America. The message was called forth by a suspicion that some of the powers of Europe were seeking to gain control over the South American states which had recently freed themselves from Spanish rule and become independent.

In the closing year of Monroe's term of office La Fayette on invitation from the government visited once more the United States. He was received everywhere with the honors he so richly merited from the great services he had rendered the country fifty years before, and when his year's stay was over he returned to France in a frigate which bore his name and with a present from Congress of two hundred thousand dollars and a township of public land.

COTTON PLANT.

CHAPTER XX.

THE "AMERICAN SYSTEM" AND NULLIFICATION.

THERE were four candidates for the presidency in 1824, all of them Republicans (Democrats), for the Federalist party had ceased to exist and the Whig party had not yet come into being. Of these Andrew Jackson received the most electoral votes, but not a majority, and so for a second time the House of Representatives was called upon to choose the President. There the friends of two of the other candidates combined against Jackson and secured the election of John Quincy Adams.

John Quincy Adams was the first President who had had no part in either the Revolutionary War or in framing the Constitution. He had come into public life after the Constitution was adopted and the new government organized under it. A son of John Adams, he had first served his country as Minister to the Netherlands and to Prussia, then as United States Senator, then as Minister to Russia and then as Monroe's Secretary of State. It is a curious fact that four of the first six Presidents should have been Secretaries of State under some of their predecessors, the last three in fact going direct from that office to the executive chair.

The elder Adams was still living when his son became President, but the latter had been in office only a little more than a year when his father died. By a remarkable coincidence both he and Jefferson died on the same day, and that day (July 4, 1826) was the fiftieth anniversary of the adoption of the Declaration of Independence, of which one had been the author and the other the principal supporter. The two had been life-long friends except for a brief interval at the beginning of Jefferson's presidency, and each died in the belief that the other was still living.

The administration of Monroe had witnessed the introduction into the United States from Great Britain of lighting by gas (1822); that of the younger Adams saw another invention brought from over the Atlantic which proved of infinitely more value and which rivalled in importance even Fulton's steamboat. This was the railroad, first tried in England in 1825, and in America, at Quincy (Mass.) and at Albany, in 1827. In the course of a few years railroads were built through most of the settled parts of the United States and proved a most powerful help in enabling us to make use of the natural wealth of the country and in enlarging its settlements.

Without question, the locomotive steam-engine has done more for the prosperity of America than any other one thing that can be named. It has hastened by at least a quarter of a century the development of the vast region northwest of the Mississippi. It has made it possible for the people in every section of the country to obtain quickly and cheaply the products of every other section. More than all, it has so encouraged the inhabitants of one State to travel and mingle among those of other States that

JOHN QUINCY ADAMS.

it has knit the whole people into one nation as probably nothing else would have done.

Though the benefits which were to be derived from the railroad were not felt immediately, the country was in a very prosperous condition, and this the protectionists claimed was the effect of the tariff of 1824. They therefore became urgent to have the duties made still higher, on the ground that such a course would result in even greater wealth to the country. This policy was advocated by Adams and his Secretary of State, Henry Clay, and they induced Congress in 1828 to pass a bill raising the imposts (or taxes on imports). The revenues which came from these increased duties were devoted to continuing the improvements of roads, canals and harbors previously begun under Monroe.

This "American system," as the combination of a protective tariff with internal improvements came to be called, proved the ruin of Adams as the "Alien and Sedition Laws" had of his father before him. It broke up the Republican party into two sections, one believing as did Adams and Clay, and the other opposed to their policy. In the latter division, which took the name of the Democratic party, was found nearly the entire South, which having no manufactories, favored free trade or at least a low tariff. The other division of the Republicans (which soon took the name of Whigs) obtained its support at the North, especially in New England, where nearly all of the manufacturing of the country was done and which accordingly desired the protection afforded by a high tariff. The North and South thus became divided to some extent on another subject besides that of the right or wrong of slavery.

HENRY CLAY.

THE FIRST STEAM-ENGINE.

Other things as well as the tariff and internal improvements entered into the party feeling of the time and helped to destroy the political quiet which had so long rested upon the nation. Adams personally was not a popular man with the people, though he was respected and even feared. Trained in politics by his father, he was felt to belong to the old school of statesmen and not to be in sufficient sympathy with the changed conditions of the country to properly be its head. But the great thing against him, that which chiefly led to his overthrow, was the sentiment that the presidency had not been fairly awarded to him in 1824, and that the man who had then received the most votes should have been President. This it was that, when he stood for re-election in 1828, caused him to be hopelessly defeated by the same candidate who had outvoted him four years before, but whom the House of Representatives had then set aside in his favor, General Andrew Jackson.

Andrew Jackson, the hero of New Orleans, "Old Hickory" as his party associates loved to call him, was not without political experience when he entered upon the presidency, though his experience had not been as extensive as that of most of his predecessors. He had been a member of both branches of Congress as well as of the Supreme Court of Tennessee, the State of his adoption though not of his birth. It was as a soldier, however, in the second war with England that he had won his distinction and shown his fitness as a natural leader of men. Honest, fearless, bold and energetic, he allowed no obstacle to prevent his doing what he thought was right or necessary.

The administration of Jackson was a stormy one. There were foreign difficulties with France. There were wars with the Indians. There was trouble with the States. There were disagreements with Congress. From the beginning to the end of his eight years' presidency Jackson was engaged almost constantly in some contest, small or great, and from every one of them he came out the victor.

His first attack was upon office-holders whose politics differed from his own, all of whom he swept from office as no President before him had done, and thus established a custom which has been followed almost without exception by each of his successors. Then he turned against the Bank of the United States, in which, since the early days of the Republic, the public money had been kept, vetoed the bill passed by Congress to renew its charter (1832), and forcibly removed the government deposits to State banks. Opposed to the "American system" of high tariff and internal improvements, he showed his disapproval by refusing to sign any of the many harbor, canal and river bills sent him by Congress.

These acts were all directed against his political opponents. But he was not afraid to proceed against his political friends, as well, when his views differed from theirs. He himself believed in a low tariff, but while a high tariff was the law he thought it should be obeyed. South Carolina, like all of the South, was opposed to protective duties. But her opposition took a more violent form than did that of other States. When Congress in 1832 again raised the tariff, South Carolina refused to obey the new law, declared it null (of no effect), forbade her citizens to pay the duties, and threatened to secede if the national government should try to enforce it. Such a defiance of federal authority Jackson was not the kind of man to tolerate. He at once sent a naval force to Charleston harbor to

ANDREW JACKSON.

collect duties from every incoming ship. He ordered troops to the interior of the State to keep order. He issued a proclamation notifying the people that the law would be carried out, whatever happened, and that if they resisted it would be at the peril of their lives. This brought South Carolina to her senses. She had not been prepared for quite so much energy. She determined to wait a little before giving effect to her "nullification," and see what Congress would do. What Congress did was to adopt a "compromise tariff" (1833), providing for a steady annual decrease in the duties, and so quieted the troubled waters.

He was equally decisive in foreign matters. Americans had long been seeking payment for the injuries done their commerce by France in the early years of the century, but without success, until Jackson threatened to seize enough French ships to make good the old loss and directed our Minister at Paris to demand his passports and come home (1834). This was sufficient. The five millions of dollars claimed by us were paid and harmony between the two nations restored.

The first of the Indian troubles was an outbreak on the part of the Sac and Fox tribes in Wisconsin (1832), led by Black Hawk, a chief whose name has been given to the war, and which resulted after a few months' contest in the removal of the Indians beyond the Mississippi. A more serious disturbance occurred a few years later in Florida with the Seminoles. It originated in the shelter they gave negro slaves who had run away and whom they refused to give up to their masters. This made the whites very desirous of getting rid of such neighbors. The war lasted seven years (1835-1842) and ended as the

BANK OF THE UNITED STATES.

Black Hawk one had done, in driving the Indians west of the Mississippi. A third Indian tribe also had to give up its lands during this period and cross the great river. This was the Cherokee tribe, which the government after some little difficulty induced to leave Alabama and Georgia in 1836.

But the tumults, quarrels and excitements of the time did not interrupt the growth or prosperity of the country, more marked perhaps during these years than at any other period in our history. Even a great fire in New York, which destroyed twenty million dollars' worth of property, did not affect the nation at large, and only briefly checked the increase of wealth in that city. In the very year of that fire (1835) the national debt was entirely paid off and Congress found itself with an income (from the tariff) larger than was needed for the expenses of the government, and it could discover no better means of using the surplus than by dividing it among the States. But the States felt as prosperous as the federal government and were spending money freely in building railroads and canals, improving highways and establishing more and better schools. Private wealth kept pace with public prosperity. The number of banks rapidly increased; more money was put into manufactories; and the sales of government lands rose from one million dollars a year to twenty-five millions. It was at this time that friction matches came into use, and that coal took the place of wood. The reaping-machine was invented in 1834 and the revolving pistol in 1835. Steamboats, which as yet had only been used on the rivers and lakes, began to cross the ocean. Imprisonment for debt began to be abolished, and the abolition of slavery began to be advocated. The temperance movement as an organized effort to restrict the use of alcoholic drink also first came to the front at this period.

The admission of Arkansas and Michigan into the Union during the last years of Jackson's term increased the number of States to twenty-six, thus just doubling the original thirteen. Arkansas had been part of the French purchase and had been included successively in the territories of Louisiana and Missouri until the latter in 1819 had formed a State government, when she was made a territory by herself under her present name (that of a former tribe of Indians). She entered the Union in 1836, and as she was south of Missouri she came in as a slave State. Michigan followed a year later as the fourth (free) State taken from the Northwest Territory, though she had had a separate territorial government of her own since 1805. Her name was taken from that given by the Indians to the body of water separating her from Wisconsin and which means "great lake." The first settlement in each of these two new States was made by the French, at Arkansas Post (1685) and at Detroit (1701) respectively, and for a long time these were about the only settlements in the two territories.

CHAPTER XXI.

VAN BUREN, HARRISON, TYLER.

MARTIN VAN BUREN.

AFTER serving for two terms Jackson in 1837 was succeeded in the presidency by Martin Van Buren. The Whigs had become discouraged by their defeats in 1828 and in 1832 (when Jackson was re-elected) and made no nomination against Van Buren, scattering their vote among a number of candidates. Their leader was Henry Clay, author of the "Missouri Compromise" and the great advocate of protective duties and internal improvements, who had twice before been a presidential candidate and each time beaten (1824 and 1832). Besides serving as Secretary of State under John Quincy Adams, Clay was for many years a member of the House of Representatives and afterwards United States Senator from Kentucky.

A native of New York, Van Buren had held a number of State offices (among them the governorship), had been a United States Senator and then in turn Secretary of State and Vice-President (under Jackson) before rising to the highest position in the gift of the nation. Both of these last (and highest) two offices he owed to the friendship of Jackson, who procured his nomination from the Democrats in gratitude for his loyal support.

But Van Buren was able to retain the presidency only one term, thus making the third President in the first fifty years of the Constitution who failed of re-election. His defeat was caused by the financial panic which swept over the country the year he took office, and of which the effect was felt during most of his term. The prosperity of the previous fifteen or twenty years had led people to extend their business beyond the needs of the country, growing as that was. To supply the money required by this expansion of trade the banks had issued notes far in excess of their ability to redeem them with gold and silver. Indeed, many of these banks had never intended to redeem them when they issued them. The failure of the banks to make good their notes when presented brought on the panic, which involved thousands in ruin. The government itself for a time was embarrassed, as the State banks in which its funds were deposited were obliged to suspend with the rest. It was on this account that Congress, at the suggestion of Van

WILLIAM H. HARRISON.

HISTORY OF THE UNITED STATES.

JOHN TYLER.

Buren, soon after established subtreasuries in various parts of the country, where the public money has since been kept safe from the danger of bank failure.

Though Van Buren can hardly be held responsible for the panic, the people did lay it partly at his door, and thought that they might find relief from the depression in business and general distress by a change in the government. Accordingly in 1840 the Whigs, for the first time since their party was formed, and after one of the most exciting campaigns in our political history, famous for the size of its meetings, the length of its processions and the quantity of "hard cider" drunk, succeeded at last in electing one of their number President, General William H. Harrison.

Harrison, like Jackson, had gained his popularity through his services in the War of 1812, but, also like Jackson, had held public office before his elevation to the presidency. By birth a Virginian, he removed to the Northwest Territory in early manhood and became one of the first territorial governors of Indiana and afterwards its representative in turn in each branch of Congress, and then was sent abroad as United States Minister to Colombia.

The triumph of the Whigs was short-lived. Scarcely a month after taking the oath Harrison died (April 6, 1841), and in his successor, chosen though he was by their votes, the Whigs found anything but a friend to their cause.

John Tyler had been elected Vice-President on the same ticket with Harrison, and so on the death of the latter became President. This was in accordance with the provisions of the Constitution, which in fact had only created the vice-presidential office in order to provide for an immediate successor to the presidency should that position become vacant by death, resignation or removal. No occasion having before this arisen for the Vice-President to assume the higher office, the position had come to be little thought of. Its duties were trifling, it exerted slight influence, and in making nominations to fill it parties looked with much more care at the votes to be obtained than at the special fitness of the candidate. It was this which had induced the Whigs to associate Tyler with Harrison at the recent election, and which had now made the former President. For though Tyler called himself a Whig, he was in reality a Democrat of the most extreme type. He was a strong believer in State sovereignty, or the right of a State to act independently of the national government and even to leave the Union if it chose. He had therefore emphatically approved of South Carolina's attempt at nullification and had bitterly opposed Jackson's course in stamping it out, and it was only to show

DANIEL WEBSTER.

his hostility to Jackson that he (nominally) left the Democratic party and became a Whig. The Whigs had placed his name on the ticket in the hope that it might attract the votes of other Southerners who thought as he did. He was from Virginia and had been governor of that State, a member of Congress and Senator.

Tyler's administration was a four years' struggle between the President and the Whigs in Congress. Nearly every bill passed by them was vetoed by him, and though they had for the first half of his term a majority in both houses it was of little avail against his opposition. All the members of his Whig cabi-

JOHN C. CALHOUN.

net soon resigned excepting Daniel Webster, Secretary of State, who remained in office to complete a treaty he was arranging with Great Britain for the extradition of criminals and the settlement of the boundary between Canada and Maine (1842). This was the first treaty ever made by the United States providing for the return of criminals to the country from which they had fled, but we now have similar treaties with nearly all civilized nations. Webster, who made the treaty, was Clay's great rival in the leadership of the Whig party. He was a Senator for many years from Massachusetts and was without dispute the foremost orator of his age. His most brilliant opponent was John C. Calhoun, who succeeded him as Tyler's Secretary of State, and who previously had been Monroe's Secretary of War and Vice-President during Jackson's first term. It was, however, while in Congress (to which he was

SAMUEL F. B. MORSE.

sent by South Carolina) that Calhoun, like Webster and Clay, won his great fame. As the most eloquent defender of slavery, the leading advocate of State sovereignty and the originator of nullifica-

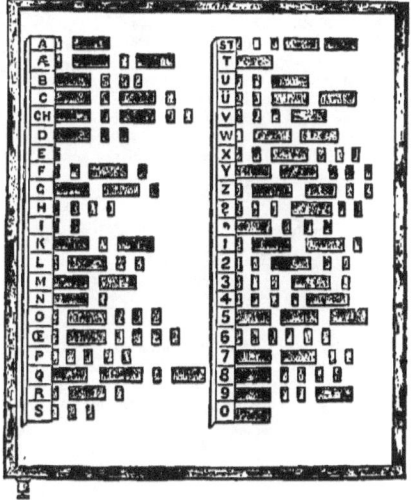

MORSE'S TRANSMITTING PLATE.

tion, he occupied for nearly twenty years before the nation the most commanding position held by any Southern man.

The most important difference between Tyler and

TRANSMITTING KEY.

Congress was on the annexation of Texas. Texas had belonged to Mexico, but in 1835 had rebelled and set up a government of its own. Many Americans had settled there, and through their efforts application was made by it for annexation to the United States. This Tyler would have been glad to do, but at first Congress would not consent. The North opposed its admission both on the slavery question and because of the probability that it would involve us in war with Mexico. The South favored it, as it would help to preserve the balance between the slave and free States, which the South feared would soon be lost to her through the increasing settlements in the (free) Northwest. The matter was discussed during all of Tyler's term and became the controlling issue in the election of his successor (1844). Then the verdict of the people was

ATLANTIC TELEGRAPH CABLE, 1866.

for admission, and in the following year she was both annexed and made a State—the last slave State to enter the Union. Florida, also a slave State, had preceded her by a few months. Though possessing the oldest settlement in the United States (St. Augustine, founded 1565), her increase in population had been slow, owing chiefly to the vast swamps which occupied so much of her territory. It was on this account that her admission as a State was delayed for nearly twenty-five years after her purchase from Spain (1821).

But Tyler's administration is to be associated with something of immensely more consequence than the annexation of Texas or the extradition treaty. In the year that he went out of office the third greatest invention that the world has known — with which only printing and the steam-engine can be compared — was perfected and put into operation. Samuel

MORSE'S RECORDING TELEGRAPH.

F. B. Morse had secured patents for an electric telegraph in 1837, but it was not until 1845 that he could obtain the necessary money from Congress to show the practical usefulness of his invention. Then a line was built from Baltimore to Washington and the value of his discovery at once showed itself. Telegraphy has now come to play so important a part in the conduct of all public and private business that it is no longer possible to measure the changes it has produced or to estimate the benefits it has conferred.

CHAPTER XXII.

THE MEXICAN WAR.

The election of 1844 turned upon the annexation of Texas, the Democrats supporting it and the Whigs opposing it. The former won and their candidate, James K. Polk, accordingly became President in 1845. Clay for the third time had received the nomination of his party and for the third time had been defeated.

Polk was born in North Carolina, but at the age of ten removed to Tennessee, of which he later became Representative in Congress and afterwards Governor. He served but one term, and of this the great event was the Mexican War.

Mexico had never acknowledged the independence of Texas, and felt aggrieved at the action of the United States in annexing it while still regarded by her as a rebellious province. This feeling of soreness was further increased by a disagreement as to its western boundary. A strip of land lying between the Nueces and Rio Grande rivers was claimed by both the Texans and the Mexicans. President Polk upheld the claim of the former and sent General Zachary Taylor to take possession of the disputed territory. This the Mexicans resented, as they considered it an invasion of their country, and a body of their soldiers crossing the Rio Grande attacked and overcame a small troop of American cavalry (April 26, 1846). Congress thereupon declared (May 13) that Mexico had begun war and voted the necessary money and men for carrying it on. Though the Whigs did not approve of the war as having been needlessly commenced by the President (and not by Mexico), they did not oppose granting the money, as they thought that the soldiers already sent to the frontiers should be protected.

The war thus begun was an almost unbroken series of victories for the Americans, whose discipline, equipment and good leadership enabled them to overcome in nearly every battle greatly superior numbers. Taylor soon drove the Mexicans back over the Rio Grande and gained control of the tract of land in question. California (then Mexican territory) was conquered with little difficulty during the same summer (1846) by a fleet sent around to the Pacific, assisted by land forces under Frémont, then in the West exploring Oregon. At the same time what is now New Mexico was seized by General Kearny, who led a body of troops there over-

land from Kansas. This gave the United States possession of all the provinces of Mexico excepting those which still belong to her, and the rest of the war was entirely waged within her present boundaries.

In the latter part of 1846 Taylor with some six thousand men moved into northern Mexico and on Sept. 24 stormed and captured Monterey in the face

JAMES K. POLK.

of odds of nearly two to one. The following February he won a yet more brilliant victory at Buena Vista. His force, which after the battle of Monterey had been increased to nine thousand men, was now reduced (by reinforcements sent to assist General Scott in an expedition against central Mexico) to five thousand men, of whom nearly all were fresh recruits untried in battle. In this condition he was met by Santa Anna, the Mexican commander-in-chief, with an army of twenty thousand men. Taylor was able to place his men to advantage at the head of a steep mountainous pass (Buena Vista), where they could only be attacked in front. Santa Anna charged the leaving two thousand dead behind him (Feb. 24, 1847).

BATTLE OF BUENA VISTA.

Americans again and again, but was beaten back each time, and at length after a day spent in fruitless attempts to dislodge them from their position was compelled to abandon the contest and to retire,

While General Taylor was operating in northern Mexico, General Winfield Scott was proceeding against the central portion of the country with a view to ending the war by capturing the City of

THE MEXICAN WAR.

Mexico. Crossing the Gulf of Mexico in March, 1847, with a force of thirteen thousand men, he attacked Vera Cruz, and after more than a week's cannonading captured it (March 27) with five thousand prisoners and five hundred pieces of artillery. He then set out with nine thousand men for the capital, defeating the enemy wherever he met them, but fighting no important battle excepting that of Cerro Gordo, where he was opposed by Santa Anna at the head of twelve thousand Mexicans, whom he badly routed, taking three thousand of them prisoners. Resting on high land for a while during the hot and sickly summer months, he took up his march again in August and soon reached the borders of the valley where the city lay. Making a new road for themselves around the fortifications built to defend the valley, the Americans began the descent of the mountain side and met with no serious delay until they arrived within ten miles of the city. There a more resolute attempt was made to check them and in one day (August 20) they fought five battles and were victorious in all.

The Mexicans then took refuge in the city, leaving Scott in possession of pretty much everything outside with the exception of the fortress of Chapultepec, situated on a steep hill, and a smaller fort below it called Molino del Rey. The latter was easily captured, but more trouble was found in taking the former, as its position rendered it difficult of access. The Americans finally effected an entrance

SANTA ANNA.

through the windows by the use of scaling-ladders, and after a stubborn resistance compelled its surrender (Sept. 13). Then they turned at once upon the city and attacked it upon an unexpected side.

CITY OF MEXICO.

Santa Anna with the remnant of his army fled, and on Sept. 14, 1847, Scott entered and the American flag floated over the capital of Mexico.

SAN FRANCISCO IN 1849.

There were a few skirmishes after this in other parts of the country, but the war was virtually ended with the capture of the City of Mexico, though the treaty of peace was not signed until the following February (1848). By it the United States not only gained the strip of land which had caused the war but also the territory now included in California, Nevada, Utah, Arizona and New Mexico, as well as part of Colorado and Wyoming. For the cession of this land Mexico received fifteen millions of dollars in money and the assumption by Congress of a debt of three and a half millions of dollars which she owed to American citizens. Though she had made but little use of them and they were very thinly settled, Mexico was very reluctant to give up these provinces. But the Americans were determined to have them on account of the fertility of the Californian soil and the fine harbor afforded by San Francisco Bay, and in fact it was only to compel Mexico to sell them that the war had been prolonged beyond the first few months.

When the terms of the sale were made neither party knew of the special value the purchase was to prove to the buyer. No one dreamed there was gold in California until just two weeks before the treaty was formally signed, when it was accidentally discovered on the banks of the Sacramento River (Jan. 19, 1848). At first the news was received with the greatest doubt, but when it was once clearly proved to be true the wildest excitement prevailed. Men hastened from all parts of the country and even from Europe to the gold-fields, and in less than two years the population of California had risen from fifteen thousand to one hundred thousand inhabitants.

The Mexican War was not the only foreign difficulty in Polk's time. There was also a disagreement with Great Britain. Webster in 1842 had settled the northern boundary between Canada and the United States as

GOLD-WASHERS IN CALIFORNIA.

far west as the Rocky Mountains, but had been unable to arrange that between the Oregon country and British Columbia. England claimed as far south as the Columbia River; the United States as far north as latitude 54° 40'. American settlement of the region had already begun and the feeling with many was very strong not to give up any of the claim, but if necessary to go to war to defend it. Their cry was, "Fifty-four forty or fight." Fortunately moderate counsels prevailed and in 1846 the question was adjusted by selecting a middle line as the boundary.

While the negotiations for this boundary treaty were in progress the twenty-ninth State was being admitted into the Union. Iowa (an Indian name) had been part of the Louisiana purchase, and was the fourth State formed from that tract. There had been an attempt at settlement by the French towards the close of the last century, but this had failed and it was not until after the Black Hawk War (1832) that the real settlement had begun. Two years later (1848) Wisconsin (which also takes its name from the Indians) had followed Iowa, and was the fifth and last State into which the Northwest Territory was divided. A few small settlements had been founded within her borders by the French in the seventeenth century, but they were of little account, and, like Iowa, she had made no actual progress towards development until within the preceding twenty years. The Missouri Compromise and the Ordinance of 1787 made both of these free States.

The year of Iowa's admission, of the commencement of the Mexican War and of the settlement of the northwest boundary, was also the year of the invention of the sewing-machine by Elias Howe and of the first use of ether in medicine to render patients unconscious while undergoing surgical operations. In the same year (1846) a new tariff bill was passed in which protective duties were entirely done away with and the taxes laid simply with a view to revenue. This was a victory for the free traders, who were in control at the time of all branches of the government. Their system was followed until the outbreak of the Civil War (1861), when the necessity for increased taxation furnished an opportunity, which was made use of, for accompanying it with protective features.

CHAPTER XXIII.

THE ANTI-SLAVERY STRUGGLE.

THE purchase of California brought the slavery question once more to the front as the annexation of Texas had done three years before, and again that question exerted great influence in deciding a presidential election. Mexican law did not recognize slavery and hence it did not exist in the territory ceded to the United States. The soil being already free, the anti-slavery men of the North wished it to remain so, while Southern planters were equally desirous that their favorite institution should be permitted in the new States to be formed in time from the purchase. As early as 1846, in the opening days of the war, when the acquisition of California was first contemplated, Congress began to consider this matter and it was not settled when the territory was bought or when the time for the election of Polk's successor arrived. At that election neither the Whigs nor the Democrats, for fear of losing some of their supporters, were willing to take decided ground on the question and so slavery was not mentioned in the platform of either party. But it was mentioned in the platform of a new party which first appeared at this time and which was formed solely to oppose the extension of slavery. This was the Free-soil party, whose nominee for President (1848) was Martin Van Buren. The Free-soilers did not succeed in electing Van Buren, but they drew away enough votes from the Democrats to give the presidency to General Taylor.

General Zachary Taylor, the twelfth President of the United States and the second of the only two elected by the Whigs, was a soldier by profession and had passed all of his life, since he reached manhood, in the armies of his country. He had gained distinction in the War of 1812, in the Black Hawk War, and in the War with the Seminoles before his brilliant victories at Monterey and at Buena Vista had made him the idol of his party. He was the first President who had held no political office before entering the White House, as the Executive Mansion at Washington is popularly called. In the latter part of his life he had made his home in Louisiana, but he was a native of Virginia, thus making the seventh President who could claim the Old

98 HISTORY OF THE UNITED STATES.

Dominion as the place of his birth or residence, and which gave that State the proud name of "the mother of Presidents."

But the Whigs were unfortunate. Again their President died in office (July 9, 1850), and again the reins of government fell into the hand of the Vice-President, though luckily this time he was a man more in sympathy with their ideas than Tyler had been. Millard Fillmore, whom Taylor's death promoted to the presidency, had been a member of Congress and Comptroller of New York (his own State) before his name had been joined with Taylor's on the electoral ticket in 1848. Though a life-long Whig he had never been a leader of his party, and as President he made but little mark on the history of his time.

The population of California increased so rapidly after the discovery of its gold-fields that it had not long been United States territory before it was demanding the privileges of statehood. This compelled a decision on the much debated and long delayed question of its slavery position. After another year's discussion the matter was at last settled in a way suggested by Clay, who was still in the Senate and who was a great believer in arranging disagreements by compromise. Clay's plan was to

MILLARD FILLMORE.

ZACHARY TAYLOR.

gratify the North by admitting California as a free State and at the same time please the South by adopting a new and more rigid fugitive slave law. Other disputes were also disposed of in the same act, which was thus of a very mixed character and was named the "Omnibus Bill." Congress approved of the measure, and accordingly in September, 1850, California entered the Union as the thirty-first State.

The compromise worked well in every respect excepting that in regard to fugitive slaves. But this proved a very important exception. A somewhat similar law had been on the statute-books since the foundation of the government, but hitherto it had not been very vigorously enforced. The new law, directing United States officials to arrest runaways wherever found and hand them over to their masters, was carried out with great strictness and often with considerable harshness and cruelty. It was a law, moreover, which could be, and doubtless was, many times abused in the seizure of negroes who always had been free and bearing them off into bondage on the pretext that they were escaped slaves. Such negroes were not allowed to testify in their own behalf, and so often were without any means of proving that they never had been slaves. The law had been framed principally for application in the free States, where naturally fugitive slaves would be most apt to take refuge, and its execution both upon actual runaways and free negroes gave a shock to the moral sentiment of the North as nothing else had done. For the first time it seemed to appreciate what the evils of slavery really were, and a deep and growing indignation was aroused that Northern leaders should ever have allowed Congress to pass such an act. The anti-slavery cause was helped more in a few months by the operation of this law than the Abolitionists had been able to advance it in twenty years of preaching. Northern feeling now began to turn towards ridding the country of slavery altogether instead of only restricting it, and this was what the Abolitionists had long been striving for.

The first effect of this changing sentiment in the North showed itself in the break-up of the Whig party. The anti-slavery men left it in dissatisfaction at its approval of the fugitive slave law, and this caused its Southern members also to withdraw and join the Democrats, who were more in accord with their views on what every one saw was to be the great issue for some years before the people—and that was the relation of slavery to the Union. The anti-slavery men did not at first see how they could give effect to their ideas, and so for a while their political influence was little felt. As a consequence, in 1852, Franklin Pierce, the Democratic presidential candidate, received more than five-sixths of the electoral votes cast.

Pierce was from New Hampshire, and had been successively a Representative in Congress and United States Senator; winning also some distinction afterwards in the Mexican War, which he entered as a volunteer and from which he emerged as a brigadier-general. During his administration the slavery contest continued to be the most absorbing topic of public interest.

Kansas and Nebraska were the objects in the next stage of the great struggle. Their settlement had begun and it became necessary to provide for them territorial governments. They were part of the Louisiana purchase, and so by the Missouri Compromise their soil should be free. But this the South was determined if possible to prevent, as it would surely increase the anti-slavery vote later on when the time came for their admission as States. Taking advantage, therefore, of their complete control of all branches of the government, the democrats in 1854 repealed the Missouri Compromise and enacted that the people in each Territory should decide for themselves whether or not slavery should be permitted within its boundaries.

The North looked upon this act as a deliberate breach of faith on the part of the South, and it excited even deeper indignation than the fugitive

FRANKLIN PIERCE.

slave law had done. The anti-slavery men resolved, however, that the South should not profit by it, and large numbers of Free-soilers emigrated to Kansas and Nebraska in order to form a majority of their settlers and so insure their entrance into the Union as free States. The planters were equally bent upon making them slave States, and so they likewise began to colonize the two Territories. A struggle for control began between the opposing parties which lasted for five years and in which the worst elements of human passion were displayed. Possession of the land was fought for with knife and pistol, and deeds of violence were so frequent that the Territory which first became a State was long known as "bleeding Kansas." In the end the greater numbers of the Free-soilers prevailed and secured the exclusion of slavery. A hostile Congress, however, withheld the rights of statehood until the Democrats lost control of the United States Senate by the secession of its Southern members.

The repeal of the Missouri Compromise vastly increased the ranks of those opposed to the extension

JOHN C. FRÉMONT.

of slavery and served to unite them all into one compact body which took the name of the Republican party. Its first appearance was in 1854, when it elected a majority of the House of Representatives. Two years later it put a presidential candidate into the field, John C. Frémont; but though it had grown wonderfully during the short period of its existence, it was not yet strong enough to elect a President, and Frémont was defeated by his Democratic opponent, James Buchanan.

James Buchanan, the only Pennsylvanian who has been President, had represented his native State in both houses of Congress, had been a member of Polk's Cabinet (Secretary of State) and Minister both to Russia and Great Britain before he entered upon the duties of the highest office of all. He was an accomplished lawyer and had a profound knowledge of politics, but he did not possess sufficient force of character to contend with the exceptional difficulties of the time, which day by day were driving the two sections of the country further apart.

Three more States were created during his term: Minnesota in 1858, Oregon in 1859, and Kansas in 1861. The settlement of the first of these (part of the Louisiana tract) had been long delayed by Indian occupation of the soil, but in 1851 the red men consented to give up their land to the whites, and in a few years her population had become large enough for her to enter the Union. The Californian gold-fever had hastened the settlement of Oregon, begun a few years before, by drawing people there in the hope that the precious metal might also be found within her boundaries. Some gold was discovered there, but agriculture soon proved to be much more profitable than mining, and she has since become one of our great wheat-growing States. Kansas was ready for statehood three years before it was granted her, but she did not receive it until the closing days of Buchanan's administration and until the country was on the eve of Civil War.

But before any of these new States entered the Union another financial panic swept over the country (1857) and involved many people in ruin. It was largely caused by the building of railroads in the West more rapidly than they were needed. They therefore at first did not pay their expenses and their builders became bankrupt. The failure of those who had invested their money in these railroads caused the failure of others, and so the distress spread from one class to another until nearly every one was to some degree affected. The general loss was greater than in the panic of 1837, but it was not as severely felt, as the country was richer and so could bear it better.

For the country had been growing much richer during all these years. The nine and a half millions of people in 1820 had become thirty and a half millions in 1860, worth over $15,000,000,000 in property. California was yielding an amount of gold which was soon to exceed that previously possessed by all the rest of the world. The discovery of one precious metal was followed ten years later (1858) by the discovery in Nevada of the other, and in less than twenty-five years two hundred and fifty millions of dollars' worth of silver have already been taken from the Comstock mines alone. Other discoveries of natural wealth followed close on the heels of gold and silver, among which scarcely any has been more valuable or useful than that of petroleum ("rock oil"), first found in Pennsylvania in 1859. New inventions for use in the arts, manufactures and agriculture were constantly perfected and added no less to the wealth of the country than the discovery and development of its natural resources were doing.

The increase in the prosperity of the nation, however, was much greater in the North and West than in the South. Commerce and manufactures did not thrive alongside of slavery and were almost entirely confined to the free States, which were growing rich and strong fast, while the progress of the slave States was slow. The immense number of immigrants that each year reached our shores, and of whom by far the larger part were workingmen, preferred to seek their bread where all labor was equal rather than by the side of bondmen, and so few of them turned to the South. Already the population of the free States greatly exceeded that of the slave States and it was manifestly destined to exceed it still more within a very few years, owing to the rapid settlement of the new Western States. It did not require much foresight for the South therefore to see that it would soon be hopelessly outvoted by the North.

This would not have been of so much importance if matters had remained as they were during the first fifty years of our national history. As long as the interests of all parts of the country were pretty much the same and both Northern and Southern men were found in the same political party it was of comparatively little consequence which section of the country was the larger. But the moment anything occurred to set one section against the other, the size of each and the number of votes it could cast became of the utmost importance. Such a time was approaching. The slavery question was separating the two sections. As yet the division was not complete, for a number of the Northern States which were Democratic voted with the South. But the rapid growth of the Republican party showed how probable it was that the South would soon lose this support and all the free States be united against the slave States. When that did come to pass the South knew that its political power would be forever gone, and that it would be helpless to resist the North in either preventing the extension of slavery or in abolishing it altogether. Rather than this should happen the Southern lead-

JAMES BUCHANAN.

ers preferred secession, and they began quietly to prepare for it in case the next election should go against them.

The breach between the two parts of the country was further widened early in Buchanan's term (1857) by a decision of the Supreme Court of the United States that Congress had no power to prohibit slavery in the Territories. Though this decision was in the interest of the South it did not help her cause, as the North refused to be bound by it, holding that it was clearly against the spirit of the Constitution and that the right had been exercised by Congress with the consent of all for nearly forty years.

102   HISTORY OF THE UNITED STATES.

JOHN BROWN.

The result of the Dred Scott decision (so called from the name of the person who brought the suit) therefore was only to make the North even more bitter against slavery than it had been when the fugitive slave law was put into operation and the Missouri Compromise repealed.

Two years later the South in turn was roused by an attempt made by a few extreme Abolitionists to raise an insurrection among the slaves. It was planned by John Brown, a Kansas Free-soiler, who had been driven half mad by the troubles in that territory. He led a small party into Virginia and seized some arms belonging to the United States government at Harper's Ferry with the intention of giving them to the negroes. Virginia and Maryland troops quickly overpowered the party, and Brown with five of his associates was hung. The North strongly denounced Brown's raid, but the South could not but believe that it was approved if not encouraged and aided by a large number of Northern Republicans. And thus another link was added to the chain which was steadily drawing the two sections asunder.

CHAPTER XXIV.

OUTBREAK OF THE CIVIL WAR.

Thus far the Northern Democrats had supported the views of their Southern brethren, not so much because they themselves believed in slavery as be-

STEPHEN A. DOUGLAS.

cause they had been taught to think that its existence was absolutely necessary to the South, and also because they felt that each State ought to have the right to decide for itself whether or not it

wished its soil to be free. But the claim made by the South after the Dred Scott decision, that Congress not only could not forbid slavery in the Terri-

JOHN C. BRECKENRIDGE.

tories but that it was bound to uphold it wherever a master chose to take his slaves, was more than the Democrats of the North were ready to accept, and accordingly in 1860 the party split into two di-

OUTBREAK OF THE CIVIL WAR.

visions and each section, Northern and Southern, put forward a presidential candidate, Stephen A. Douglas and John C. Breckenridge. As a result

JOHN BELL.

of this Democratic quarrel the Republican nominee, Lincoln, was elected. There was also a fourth candidate in the field who received a few votes, John Bell, who represented a small party (the American or "Know Nothing") which was opposed to unrestricted immigration.

Abraham Lincoln, the best loved of all our Presidents, excepting always Washington, was a Kentuckian by birth, but early in life removed to Indiana, and then to Illinois. Compelled by poverty to support himself from boyhood, he educated himself and worked his way from the position of a common farm laborer and rail splitter to that of a successful lawyer. The only office previously held by him was that of member of Congress, but he narrowly missed an election to the United States Senate in 1858, his successful opponent being Douglas, the leader of the Northern Democracy, whom he in turn had now defeated in the presidential race.

The South looked upon the election of Lincoln as the death-blow to any hope of extending slavery beyond its present limits and as even imperilling the future existence of slavery itself. Southern leaders thereupon began to arrange for carrying out the plans previously formed of seceding from the Union and establishing a new government, composed of the slave States, independent of the United States. South Carolina was the first to act and on Dec. 20, 1860, passed an "ordinance of secession." Mississippi, Alabama, Florida, Georgia

ABRAHAM LINCOLN.

and Louisiana followed in January, 1861, and Texas in February. Thus before Lincoln actually began his administration (March 4, 1861) seven States had declared themselves no longer members of the Union.

The South had claimed for many years that the Union was only a compact or alliance among the States, which any of them could end whenever it desired to do so. The North asserted the Union to be much more than this: that by the adoption of the Constitution the individual States had given up their sovereignty and had become only parts of one nation. It therefore denied the right of secession and considered it but another name for rebellion.

LINCOLN'S EARLY HOME IN GENTRYVILLE, IND.

February 4, 1861, delegates from the seven seceding States organized (at Montgomery, Ala.) a new government under the name of the Confederate

JEFFERSON DAVIS.

States of America and elected Jefferson Davis President and Alexander H. Stephens Vice-President. Davis was one of the prime movers in bringing about secession. He had been an officer in the army, Secretary of War under Pierce, and United States Senator from Mississippi. Stephens on the contrary had opposed secession, but like most

THE CONFEDERATE FLAG.

Southerners he felt that his State had a stronger claim upon his allegiance than the Union had, and so when Georgia adopted the ordinance he cast in his fortunes with her.

LINCOLN REVIEWING THE TROOPS IN WASHINGTON.

INTERIOR AND FLAG OF FORT SUMTER AFTER THE BOMBARDMENT.

Members of the United States Cabinet, Senators, Congressmen, clerks in the departments and officers of the army, who were citizens of the seven Confederate States, with very few exceptions resigned their positions when their States seceded and returned to their homes. Government property in the rebellious States was taken possession of by the secession authorities and United States officials were not allowed to perform their duties. Forts and arsenals belonging to the national government were seized and the arms contained in them used to equip Southern troops. Only Fort Sumter in Charleston harbor and Fort Pickens at Pensacola escaped, and the former did not long continue an exception, as it was captured by force soon after Lincoln entered upon the presidency and before he could succeed in relieving it.

Two months remained of Buchanan's term when the secession movement actively began, but he did nothing to prevent it. Nor would he allow any resistance to be made to the seizure of federal property in the Southern States. When Lincoln, therefore, took charge of affairs he found that the authority of the United States had come to a complete stop in these seven States and that no preparations whatever had been made on the part of the North for the coming struggle.

At first peaceable means, efforts at compromise, were made to induce the secessionists to abandon their attempt at forming a separate government and to resume their place in the Union. These failing, the President and Congress determined that the integrity of the country must be maintained at any cost and the rebellion put down by force. Lincoln thereupon called for seventy-five thousand volunteer soldiers (April 15), and the call was had not believed in the wisdom of secession and as yet had taken no part in it. They were, however, advocates of the right of secession if any State saw fit to exercise the right, and they strongly opposed the idea that a State could be compelled to remain in the Union against its will, or that force should

THE SIXTH MASSACHUSETTS REGIMENT IN BALTIMORE.

eagerly responded to by many times that number of men in the North and West whose blood had been roused by South Carolina's bombardment of Fort Sumter and its surrender three days before.

While Lincoln's proclamation for volunteers excited the patriotism of the North, it had exactly the contrary effect in the border States. These States be used in an attempt to hold a State. Virginia, North Carolina, Tennessee, and Arkansas, accordingly, when called upon by the President to furnish their proportion of troops to crush the rebellion, refused, preferring to throw in their lot with the seceders by withdrawing from the Union and joining the Confederacy. Though there were many seces-

OUTBREAK OF THE CIVIL WAR.

sionists in the other three slave States (Missouri, Kentucky and Maryland) they were not in a majority, so that those States remained loyal. Thus when hostilities began there were eleven Confederate and twenty-three Union States.

The first gun of the war was that fired at Fort Sumter; the first blood was that shed on April 19 when a mob in Baltimore attacked a Massachusetts regiment on its way to the defence of Washington. This was, however, nothing but a street fight and did not prevent the capital's soon becoming thoroughly well protected. No real battle occurred for several months, though a few minor skirmishes took place in the meantime. Richmond, after the secession of Virginia, was made the capital of the Confederacy, and its capture at once became the great object of Northern plans as being the surest way, it was thought, to speedily end the war. Urged on by public clamor, but against his own judgment, Lieutenant-General Winfield Scott (the federal commander-in-chief) sent General McDowell with some thirty thousand men to make the

G. T. BEAUREGARD.

attempt. But the South had realized just as keenly as the North the importance of its capital and had amply arranged for its defence. When, therefore, McDowell reached Bull Run (a small stream crossing the Richmond road thirty odd miles from Washington) he found a Confederate army about the size of his own, under command of General Beauregard, awaiting him, and there was fought (July 21) the first battle of the war. The result was disastrous to the Union cause, for though McDowell at first seemed to have the best of it, Beauregard later in the day was reënforced by General A. S. Johnston

IRVIN McDOWELL.

at the head of ten thousand men and this decided the victory in his favor. The federal troops gave way and retreated to Washington.

In some smaller engagements, as well as at Bull Run, the results of the first year were not encouraging to the North and showed that the war would not be finished in the three months hoped for. Both sides found their opponents better fighters than had been expected and so each had to prepare for a longer contest than either at the start had anticipated. The advantages of the situation, however, lay nearly all with the North. It had greater territory, a larger population and more wealth to draw upon in carrying on the struggle. Moreover, as the scene of the conflict was in the enemy's country its own land escaped the ravages of war. On the other hand the very fact that the South was the theatre of the war was in one way a help to the Confederates, as it gave them the feeling that they were fighting in defence of their own homes and firesides. Another circumstance at first in their favor was that Southern men as a rule were more accustomed to out-door life and were more fond of active sports than were the men of the North, and so more quickly adapted themselves to the soldier's life; but this was an advantage which did not last long.

Though the North gained no great victory during 1861, it prepared itself for winning victories in the future by gathering together necessary military stores, purchasing steamers for use as war vessels, erecting forts and enlisting soldiers. Disunionists in Missouri were driven from that State, and western Virginia, where there were few slave-owners and whose inhabitants in the main were loyal, was also freed from the disaffected. A line was drawn around the seceding States and guarded by Northern troops, thus confining the Confederates pretty strictly to their own territory. The federal position was still further strengthened by blockading with naval vessels the Southern ports, so that soon almost the entire Confederacy was surrounded by Union land and sea forces.

The advancing age of General Scott caused him before the close of 1861 to resign his commission and to retire from the army. The command was thereupon given to General George B. McClellan, who had made the greatest success of this first year in securing and holding possession of western Virginia. McClellan proceeded to Washington and at once devoted himself to drilling and organizing the large number of raw recruits who had hastily been mustered into service and hurried to the national capital, and by the end of the year he had converted this great mass of untrained citizens into a disciplined army of a hundred and fifty thousand soldiers.

GEORGE B. McCLELLAN.

CHAPTER XXV.

EVENTS OF 1862.

THE events of 1862, though not decisive in their result, were on the whole favorable to the North, and it occupied a stronger position at the close of the year than it held at the beginning. The line around the Confederates was drawn yet tighter and their operations confined still more rigidly within its limits. A stricter blockade of Southern ports was established and maintained. Control over most of the Mississippi River was secured. The greater part of Tennessee was reclaimed. New Orleans and some other important places were captured. And every effort made by the Confederates to break through the besieging Union armies was frustrated and repulsed. Much territory was gained by the North and none lost. But the capture of Richmond, the thing most desired of all, seemed no nearer when the year ended than when it commenced.

When the year opened it found half a million volunteers enlisted in the service of the United States. These were divided into various armies and stationed at different points around the Confederacy. The largest of these divisions was the Army of the Potomac (under the immediate command of McClel-

DON CARLOS BUELL.

lan), encamped in the neighborhood of Washington, where it had been collected both for the defence of the national capital and for an advance upon Richmond. Another important division (commanded by Gen. Don Carlos Buell) was placed in Kentucky with the object of regaining Tennessee and of aiding in opening up the Mississippi River. The control of that river was important to the Unionists, as their possession of it would divide the Confederacy by separating Arkansas, Louisiana and Texas from the other seceding States.

Buell's campaign was largely successful. Aided by Grant (who was soon to become the hero of the war) he defeated the Confederate army, which under Gen. A. S. Johnston was guarding the northern frontier of Tennessee, in a number of battles and finally drove it from the State. The most serious of these battles was that of Shiloh (or Pittsburg Landing), fought on the banks of the Tennessee River on April 6. Grant was awaiting there the arrival of Buell when he was attacked by Johnston at the head of forty thousand men. Taken wholly by surprise, the Union troops at first fell back, but their gunboats checked the enemy after its first advance and gave Grant an opportunity to

A. S. JOHNSTON.

rally his men. While the battle was still in progress, part of Buell's army reached him and with its aid he drove the enemy from the field, though not

GUNBOATS PASSING BEFORE VICKSBURG.

110   HISTORY OF THE UNITED STATES.

until after Johnston had been killed. Grant's loss was thirteen thousand out of a total of fifty-seven thousand engaged. The Confederate dead numbered eleven thousand.

Forts Henry and Donelson (on the Tennessee and Cumberland Rivers respectively) had fallen into federal hands before the battle of Shiloh, the first taken by Admiral Foote and the second by Grant, and the capture (May 30) of Corinth in the northern part of the State of Mississippi soon after that battle cleared the Mississippi as far south as Memphis. Though the Confederate General Bragg

Fort Pulaski at the mouth of the Savannah River also surrendered. Hatteras Inlet, Port Royal and some minor points on the coast had fallen to the North in 1861 and had been among its few suc-

BRAXTON BRAGG.

cesses of that year. The task of blockading Southern ports thus became much easier, as nearly all of the prominent places on the Atlantic seaboard were now in federal hands, Charleston and Wilmington being the principal exceptions.

Another naval expedition besides that of Burnside and Goldsborough was also sent out in February to attack a much more important point than

ADMIRAL FOOTE.

later in the year raided Tennessee (as well as Kentucky), he did not succeed in holding anything but a part of eastern Tennessee, the rest of the State remaining for the balance of the war under the military control of the United States.

While Buell and Grant were thus busy in Tennessee, other leaders were doing equally good work further south. Roanoke Island (North Carolina) was taken by General Burnside and Commodore Goldsborough in February, and St. Augustine and other Florida cities were captured a little later on by another body of Union troops. On April 11

A. E. BURNSIDE.

either Roanoke Island or Fort Pulaski. It was under command of Commodore Farragut and General Benjamin F. Butler, and had for its object the capture of New Orleans. The value of that city as commanding the entrance to the Mississippi was fully appreciated by both sides, and the Confederates had spared no pains in providing it with the most elaborate defences. On the opposite banks of the Mississippi some distance below New Orleans were two strong forts and stretched between them were heavy chains, resting on masses of timber. Back of the chains were placed floating batteries, fire rafts and gunboats. Along the shores from the forts to the city were other batteries. For the protection of the city itself ten thousand soldiers had been collected within its walls.

On April 18 the attack was begun by a bombardment of the forts which was kept up for nearly a week, but without avail. Farragut then decided to force a way through the obstructions in the river despite the forts and the enemy's boats. Selecting a dark night he sent a few of his gunboats ahead to cut the chains and open a passage, following himself soon after with the rest of his fleet. The heavy guns of the forts and the batteries on the banks poured a steady and murderous fire upon him as he advanced, but he passed them in safety, fought and destroyed the river fleet, and on April 25 New Orleans was taken. The surrender of the forts quickly followed, and the lower Mississippi as well as the upper was once more under Union control, leaving Vicksburg and Port Hudson the only points on the river which remained to the Confederates. They for the present were safe, as they were situated on bluffs too high to be successfully attacked by gunboats.

JOHN ERICSSON.

Before New Orleans surrendered, before even the attack upon it had commenced, the North had been confronted by a novel and unexpected danger, which looked for the moment as though it

MONITOR.

IRONCLAD GUNBOAT.

might prove a fatal one. Up to the outbreak of the Civil War ironclad vessels had never been used as ships of war, indeed they had scarcely yet been employed for any purpose, a few only having recently been built by France and England as an experiment. When the Confederates took possession of the Norfolk navy yard on the secession of Virginia they found there a wooden frigate named the "Merrimac." By covering this with metal plates they turned it into an ironclad and made it still more formidable by fastening an iron ram to its bow. Early in March she was ready for service and proceeded at once into Hampton Roads and attacked the "Cumberland" and four other United States men-of-war which with some smaller vessels were lying there at anchor. These all found themselves powerless against her. Their shot made no impression upon her iron coat, while she could pound them at will with ball upon every quarter, or tear open their sides with her iron ram. The wooden ships were absolutely at her mercy. The "Cumberland" was sunk and the others would have shared the same fate had not darkness compelled the "Merrimac" to suspend the attack.

When the telegraph that night spread the news of the terrible destructiveness of the invincible "Merrimac" the North was struck with consternation. What was there to prevent Washington, Baltimore, Philadelphia, New York, Boston and every loyal

DOUBLE-TURRET IRONCLAD.

city from being either captured or levelled to the ground, the merchant ships and navy of the Union from being swept off the face of the ocean, and the Confederacy from overrunning and subjugating every free State?

Twenty-four hours changed this panic of fear into a shout of exultation. For while the South had been occupied in converting the "Merrimac" into an armored vessel, John Ericsson, a Swedish engineer in New York, had been as busily engaged in building an ironclad for the North. His work was also finished in March and received from him the name of "Monitor." Having been sent to the South under command of Lieutenant Worden, the "Monitor" chanced to reach Fortress Monroe (in the Hampton Roads) the very night which followed the loss of the "Cumberland." When the "Merrimac" returned the next morning (March 9) to complete her work of destruction she was attacked by the "Monitor" (her inferior in size and strength) and after a long fight was compelled to retire to Norfolk, from which she did not again venture forth. The victory of the "Monitor" not only carried joy to the North, but it revolutionized naval architecture all over the world. Every nation at once began building ironclads, and they have since almost entirely supplanted in every civilized country wooden vessels as ships of war.

In Virginia, destined from the start to be the great battle-ground of the war, matters did not run as smoothly for the North in 1862 as they did elsewhere. There was much fighting there during the year, but little came of it. Two expeditions were sent against Richmond and both failed. McClellan led the first (numbering one hundred thousand men) in the Spring by boat to Fortress Monroe and thence up the peninsula which separates the York and James Rivers. This route was chosen to avoid the bad roads and swollen and unbridged streams of the more direct one overland. But before he reached Richmond, after meeting the enemy with varying success in a number of engagements, a series of attacks upon the forces left for the defence of Washington recalled him to that city. Another effort was made by General Burnside with a still larger army later in the year. Burnside took the shortest road, but was so badly defeated at Fredericksburg (December 13) that he also had to give up the attempt.

After McClellan's return to Washington, and before Burnside started on his expedition, General Robert E. Lee, the commander-in-chief of the Confederacy, led an army north in an attempt to break through the Union lines and capture some important Northern city. McClellan threw himself in

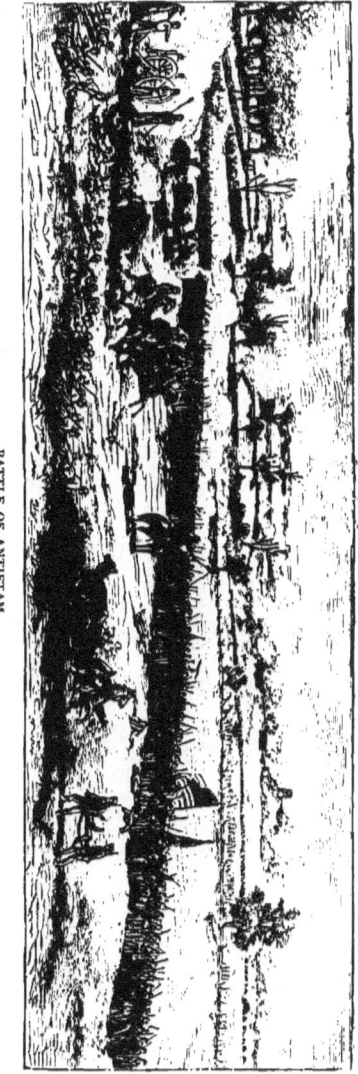

BATTLE OF ANTIETAM.

Lee's way, compelled him to turn aside from his direct path and then hastened after him. At Antietam (Maryland) the two armies met and fought one of the great battles of the war (September 17). Neither side won a decided victory, but Lee gave up his invasion and returned to Virginia.

There had been a good deal of dissatisfaction with McClellan before the battle of Antietam. He had been nearly a year in command of the Army of the Potomac, the largest, best drilled and most thoroughly equipped body of soldiers on the continent, and had accomplished nothing? To his excessive slowness and overcaution was laid the failure of the Spring campaign against Richmond and of all the other operations in Virginia. The result at Antietam, particularly his allowing Lee to escape with his army afterwards, greatly heightened the general distrust in him at Washington and determined Lincoln at last to remove him from the command. This was done and his place given to Burnside, who had so successfully conducted the expedition against Roanoke Island early in the year. Burnside, however, was able to retain it but a short time. His defeat at Fredericksburg compelled him to ask to be relieved, and about the beginning of 1863 he was succeeded by General Joseph E. Hooker.

CHAPTER XXVI.

THE THIRD YEAR OF THE WAR (1863).

THE South had gone to war to perpetuate and to extend slavery. But by going to war it brought slavery to a much more speedy end than there is any likelihood would have otherwise happened. For on January 1, 1863, the President issued an emancipa-

THOMAS J. JACKSON ("*Stonewall*").

tion proclamation which declared that all slaves in the States then in rebellion should from that time forth be considered free. Some months before doing this Lincoln had warned the seceding States that if they did not renew their allegiance to the federal government by the close of 1862 he should take this step. None of them did lay down their arms by that time, and the proclamation was accordingly made. Two years later (1865) the thirteenth Amendment to the Constitution was adopted which forever prohibited slavery within the United States.

Once again the Army of the Potomac moved towards Richmond, led this time by its new commander, General Hooker. Skirting the defences at Fredericksburg, it had advanced about ten miles on its way when it met the Confederates under Lee and Jackson at Chancellorsville. The Union forces were twice the number of their enemy, but the latter were so much better handled by their generals that they drove Hooker back (May 2 and 3, 1863) with a loss of seventeen thousand men out of the ninety thousand he had with him. The Confederate loss was twelve thousand, but one of these twelve thousand was worth an army in himself. This was General Jackson, Lee's ablest assistant, who had won the name of "Stonewall" from his unyielding firmness and courage at the battle of Bull Run.

His success at Chancellorsville encouraged Lee in the following month to again attempt a Northern raid. Taking some seventy thousand men, he moved to the west of Hooker's army and then turned and started for the North. Hooker followed closely after, keeping a little to the right of Lee's line of march so as to better protect Washington, Baltimore, Philadelphia and other large and important Eastern cities should the Confederates attack them. On reaching the Pennsylvania border, after crossing western

Maryland, Lee changed his course towards Philadelphia. But the Union army (now under General Meade in the place of Hooker) was near enough to interpose itself between that city and the advancing Confederates, and Lee found it awaiting him at Gettysburg. The battle which ensued was one of the most gallantly fought on both sides of any in the war. It lasted three days (July 1, 2 and 3) and cost over fifty thousand lives. The result was a victory for Meade, who again and again repulsed the attack of the Confederates and finally drove them from the field. This was the most serious reverse Lee had as yet met with. He returned to Virginia, leaving nearly half the army he had set out with dead behind him, and made no further attempt to invade the North.

Another great Union victory was won almost simultaneously with that at Gettysburg. As the last shots were being exchanged at that battle, Grant was completing the capture of Vicksburg, the most important of the two points on the Mississippi River still in Confederate hands. The close of 1862 had left Grant at Corinth, some little distance northeast of Vicksburg. Between him and that city was a large army under Generals Pemberton and J. E.

JOSEPH E. HOOKER.

Johnston, the latter being in command of all the Confederates in the West.

After several unsuccessful attempts on Vicks-

GUARDING A BRIDGE ON THE POTOMAC.

burg in other directions. Grant moved a part of his army across the river at Memphis, descended its western side and recrossed at a point a little south of the city. Pushing northeast he met Pemberton and defeated him in a number of battles and at last

GEORGE G. MEADE.

compelled him and his men to take refuge in Vicksburg. Turning then upon the army which Johnston in the meantime had been gathering together to aid Pemberton, Grant drove it back and united his forces with those which he had left behind him under General Sherman when he crossed the river. The Union army was now between Vicksburg and Johnston and at once began a close and active siege of the city. Johnston tried to relieve it but was kept at bay by Grant and so could give it no help. Unable either to escape or to obtain assistance, Pemberton, after holding out for six weeks, surrendered and on July 4 gave up the place and with it his army of thirty thousand men to Grant. Only Port Hudson now remained to the Confederates on the Mississippi, and that was not long in following Vicksburg. For as soon as the news was received of Pemberton's fate, Port Hudson hastened to make terms with General Banks, who was besieging it at the time, and on July 8 he took possession. The entire river was now completely under federal control and one of the two great objects for which the North had been striving since the very beginning of the war had at length been attained. The result was the dividing and in consequence the weakening of the Confederacy.

Of the other operations during 1863 the most important were those in Tennessee. Rosecrans was the Union commander there, and in June he

BATTLE OF GETTYSBURG.

THE THIRD YEAR OF THE WAR.

moved against Bragg, who still retained the hold on the eastern part of the State he had gained the preceding year. Bragg slowly fell back across the Georgia boundary, where he was reinforced by a part of Lee's army from Virginia. At Chickamauga (twelve miles south of Chattanooga) he halted until Rosecrans came up and then attacked him (Sept. 19). The Confederates slightly outnumbered their opponents and after a two days' battle defeated them and compelled them to retire.

Rosecrans and his men thereupon shut themselves up in Chattanooga, to which Bragg immediately laid siege.

From the latter part of September till near the end of November the siege of Chattanooga was vigorously pressed without any opportunity offering itself for the escape of those within the apparently doomed city. The Confederate army sur-

SIEGE OF VICKSBURG BY GEN. GRANT.

rounding it was large; every passable road leading to it was under Bragg's control; even the neighboring hills of Lookout Mountain and Missionary Ridge were fortified. There seemed to be no more chance of assistance reaching it from without than there was hope of its saving itself from within. Its

INTERVIEW BETWEEN GENERALS GRANT AND PEMBERTON.

only choice appeared to be between submission and starvation.

At this juncture Grant arrived. His capture of Vicksburg had fixed all eyes upon him as almost

W. S. ROSENCRANS.

the war, most of the fighting being done by guerillas, or irresponsible bodies of armed men who did not form part of the organized army and were not under control of the military authorities. What Confederate troops there were in the State were easily driven out by a force sent into it by Grant soon after the surrender of Vicksburg; after which Arkansas gave but little trouble.

On the coast matters did not go quite so well. Persistent efforts were made during a considerable part of the year to capture Fort Sumter and Charleston, but they were fruitless. The fort was battered to ruin and great damage was done to the city by the cannonading of General Gillmore, the Union commander, but he failed either to take the one or to get nearer to the other than the mouth of the river. Sabine Pass and Brownsville, on the Texan coast, were, however, captured by an expedition from New Orleans, and a naval battle was won by the monitor "Weehawken" over the "Atlanta," a Confederate ironclad, somewhat similar to the "Merrimac," but larger and stronger. As the "Atlanta" was proceeding to attack a blockading fleet at the mouth of the Savannah, she encountered the "Weehawken," to which after a sharp but brief fight of less than half an hour she had to surrender (June 17).

the only leader who thus far during the war had been uniformly successful in his campaigns, and who, many already believed, would prove to be the man to end the rebellion. He had now been placed in command of all the Western forces of the Union and had come to Chattanooga to see what could be done to relieve the beleaguered city. Collecting an army in the rear of that of Bragg, he soon formed his plan of attack. This was no less an undertaking than to surprise the Confederates by climbing the two mountains, storming the fortifications they had erected on them and from the vantage-ground thus gained, overlooking as it would Bragg's army, compel the enemy to abandon the siege.

The plan worked to a charm. The "battles above the clouds" were fought on November 23, 24 and 25, and were a decisive victory for Grant, who lost but six thousand men against ten thousand of those opposed to him. Bragg relinquished his attack upon the city and retired into Georgia. His retreat from Tennessee was immediately followed by that of General Longstreet, who had been besieging Knoxville while Bragg was before Chattanooga. This freed the entire State of Tennessee from the Confederates and they were not able afterwards to regain control of any part of it. From that day to this federal authority has been supreme throughout it.

Arkansas as well as Tennessee was this year reclaimed from the Confederacy. There had not been many regular engagements in this State during

GENERAL LONGSTREET.

CHAPTER XXVII.

NEARING THE END (1864).

THEIR defeats at Gettysburg, Vicksburg and Chattanooga were a heavy blow to the Confederates and crippled them severely. They could ill afford to spare the men lost in those battles. They could not much better dispense with the supplies they had been receiving from beyond the Mississippi and from other districts which had now passed under Union control. The war was bearing down upon the South far more cruelly than upon the North and was taxing its resources to the utmost. A large part of its men had been pressed into the Confederate armies, leaving only a comparatively small number to do the work necessary for the support of the women and children as well as for the maintenance of the soldiers themselves. Indeed often the women and children were called upon to perform labor for which they were unfit through lack of men to do it for them. The strictness of the blockade on land and sea shut out goods of every kind and compelled the Southerners to rely almost entirely for what they needed on what they could themselves produce. The absence of manufactures in the South forced the people to do without some of the most common necessities. Luxuries were unknown, Comforts were rare. The plainest food and clothing became scarce and costly. Cotton, tobacco, rice and the other articles which once found a ready sale at the North and in Europe and which made the wealth of the South now lay unsold on their owners' hands. For though occasionally a ship would successfully run the blockade, it was exceptional, and for the most part the planters were unable to find a purchaser for their products because they were unable to send them to market. What coin there was when the war began was soon exhausted and the paper money issued by the Confederate government to take its place rapidly lost its value, so that the people were often unable to buy

ULYSSES S. GRANT.

the few things which did escape the blockade through want of means to pay for them.

It was different at the North. There was no blockade of Union ports, so that goods could still be sent abroad and other goods received in return very much the same as before the war. Confederate cruisers and privateers interfered somewhat with this foreign trade and did it considerable injury, but

ROBERT E. LEE.

bear them, and did bear them patiently and cheerfully, suffering far less under their burdens than did their Southern opponents.

At the beginning of 1864 everything pointed to a speedy and successful ending of the war by the North. Union armies had split the Confederacy, taken away great slices of its territory, repelled its invasions, defeated it in battle, and were gradually confining it within a smaller and smaller space. Its lack of means and the privations it was undergoing were known to the North and encouraged the government to feel that the struggle could not last much

they were not able to stop it or even to very seriously diminish it. Northern manufactures prospered as the increased duties, which the enormous war expenses of the government made it necessary to lay upon imports, stimulated home production. The business of the free States suffered little interruption, as the scene of the conflict was so distant from the territory of most of them. And though the taxes were many and heavy, the people were able to

BENJAMIN F. BUTLER.

longer, through sheer inability of the South to sustain it.

These hopes were not to be quite fulfilled that year, but they were very nearly realized. Immense strides were made by the federal armies, and the close of 1864 saw the South so weakened that its submission, it was evident to every one, was only a question of a few weeks or at the most of a few months. This was due to Grant, well seconded by Sherman, Sheridan and Thomas, who had most ably supported him in the West and who were now to be of still greater help in the South.

JOSEPH E. JOHNSTON.

NEARING THE END (1864).

In March, 1864, the rank of Lieutenant-General, which had been allowed to lapse on the retirement of General Scott, was revived and conferred upon Grant, and with it went the command of all the land forces of the United States. Grant at once proceeded to Virginia to fight Lee and assumed immediate charge of the Army of Potomac. He left Sherman in command of the army which had been collected in Tennessee and which had followed the Confederates when they retreated to Dalton (in northern Georgia) after the battle of Lookout Mountain and who were now under J. E. Johnston in place of Bragg. Sherman had about one hundred thousand men; Grant a little over that number; Johnston some seventy-five thousand, and Lee sixty odd thousand. The two Northern armies were thus nearly double the size of the two opposing ones, and the struggle between them constituted the main events of the balance of the war.

The plan adopted by Grant was for both himself and Sherman to move against the enemy on the same day, Grant with a view to taking Richmond and Sherman for the purpose of driving Johnston out of the Georgia mountains to level ground and there battling with him. By thus acting at the same time and keeping Lee and Johnston both steadily engaged, the armies of the two latter would be prevented from aiding each other as they had sometimes done before.

May 5 was the day selected for the joint movement. Grant made his advance in three separate divisions: one under General Butler up the James River for an attack upon Petersburg, another under Generals Hunter and Sigel through the Shenandoah valley for the seizure of Lynchburg, and the third and main body under his own command by a more direct route from the Rappahannock River to the Confederate capital. The object of the first two expeditions was to threaten Richmond on the east and west and so to partially divert Lee's attention and to divide his army while Grant was leading the assault from the north.

Butler, Sigel and Hunter were unable to accomplish their part of the task. The first became blockaded on a peninsula where he could neither advance nor retreat. The other two were defeated and compelled to abandon their expedition. Grant was in a degree more successful. He gradually forced Lee back closer to Richmond, but he did not do this without much fighting and heavy losses. Lee was a really great general, especially in a defensive campaign, and protected himself and his men (who were greatly outnumbered by those under Grant) with the utmost skill, so that the ground won from him was gained with great difficulty and only by a costly expenditure of life. In the battles of the Wilderness, Spottsylvania Court-House and Cold Harbor, fought in May and June while Grant was slowly pushing his way forward, the latter lost nearly sixty thousand men and Lee not much over half that number. It is but just to add, however, that Lee's men were able to fight for the most part from behind the fortifications which had been erected to defend the approaches to Richmond in every direction, and that Grant's losses chiefly occurred in

PHILIP HENRY SHERIDAN.

attacks upon these fortifications, where his men were necessarily much exposed. But Grant was able to constantly recruit his army, which Lee could only do to a very slight extent.

Beyond Cold Harbor (a little northeast of Richmond) Grant found it almost impossible to proceed, as the defences on that side of the Confederate capital proved too strong to be carried by assault. He therefore determined to cross the James River and attempt Richmond on its southern side. This was done, but Lee at the same time moved his army into

Petersburg (twenty miles southeast of Richmond) and there again checked Grant's further progress. From Petersburg to Richmond was a series of well-constructed Confederate fortifications which Grant at various points tried to break through, but was prevented by Lee. Grant then began building opposing fortifications so as to strengthen the line he was now drawing around Richmond, an especial interest on account of its picturesque and unexpected ending. The defeat of Sigel and Hunter in the Shenandoah valley had left a road open for a raid upon Washington through Maryland. Such a raid was made in July by General Early, one of the most dashing cavalry officers in the South, but he found Washington prepared for him and he returned to Virginia unsuccessful. Soon

SHERIDAN AT CEDAR CREEK.

and the remainder of 1864 was principally devoted by him to this work and to extending his line, with the object of cutting off Lee's communications and supplies and of finally shutting him up in the city itself.

While Grant was knocking at the gates of Richmond a battle took place in the western part of Virginia which, though it had no great effect upon the course of the war, will probably always retain after his return he was attacked and defeated at Winchester by Sheridan, who had accompanied Grant to Virginia and had been placed at the head of the Union troops in the Shenandoah valley. Early watched his chance, and just a month later (Oct. 19) surprised Sheridan's army at Cedar Creek and routed it. Sheridan was away at the time, but learned the news at Winchester, twenty miles distant from the battle-field. Taking horse he rode furiously toward Cedar Creek and on his way met his flying men. Rallying them as he galloped past, as much by example as by word, he led them back to the scene of their morning's fight, and surprising Early in turn he snatched their brief victory from the Confederates before they had had an opportunity to even taste of its sweets.

In the meantime Sherman was more than carrying out his part of the joint programme assigned him by Grant. He began to move against Johnston as had been agreed, in May, but he proceeded slowly and cautiously, as he rated at their full value the great ability and sagacity of his opponent. Johnston proved himself worthy of his reputation, and only fell back as the superior numbers of Sherman's army threatened to enclose him. Neither suffered the other to gain any advantage and neither was very desirous of fighting a pitched battle in the mountains. In this manner Johnston was gradually pushed back from point to point to Atlanta, each side meeting with about the same loss in the minor engagements fought on the way. But Sherman had been advancing through a hostile country and had to have his supplies constantly forwarded to him from Chattanooga, and so, to insure receiving them, it was necessary for him as he moved ahead to continually leave guards behind to defend the road over which the supplies were to

WILLIAM T. SHERMAN.

come. This consequently weakened his army more and more, so that by the time he reached Atlanta he had not many more men with him than had Johnston. The latter had foreseen this and in

SHERMAN'S GREAT MARCH THROUGH THE HEART OF THE SOUTH.

HISTORY OF THE UNITED STATES.

JOHN B. HOOD.

fact had prolonged his retreat for this very purpose of equalizing the two armies. He was therefore now ready to fight and was about offering Sherman battle when he was suddenly removed from the command by the Confederate government, which had become impatient at his allowing Sherman to drive him back so far. His place was given to General J. B. Hood, a soldier in every respect his inferior.

On assuming command Hood at once violently attacked Sherman, but was repulsed in each of his three assaults (July). By the end of August the Union army, after much hard fighting, had made its way around to the rear of Atlanta, and on September 2 the Confederates withdrew from the city and it was taken possession of by their opponents. Hood then formed the plan of moving towards the North with his army in the hope of tempting Sherman to follow and so changing the scene of war again from Georgia back to Tennessee. Sherman did pursue him for a short distance and then returned to Atlanta, leaving Thomas, who was already in Tennessee, to look after Hood.

The forces of Thomas and Hood were about equal, the former having made considerable additions in Kentucky and Tennessee to the troops sent him by Sherman. The capture of Nashville was the first object of the Confederates, but just before reaching that city they encountered a part of the Northern army under General Schofield. Here (at Franklin) a battle was fought, but though Hood's loss was serious his progress was not stopped and he advanced and began to besiege Nashville. Scarcely was the siege fairly under way when Thomas, who was within the city, issued forth, fell upon Hood and defeated him so overwhelmingly that his army was scattered in every direction and completely disappeared (Dec. 15 and 16). Of the seventy-five thousand veteran soldiers which at the opening of this campaign Johnston had about him at Dalton hardly a corporal's guard now remained to Hood; the rest were dead, wounded or imprisoned, or else were flying for fear of capture before the horsemen of Thomas. One of the only two great armies left to the Confederacy had entirely melted away.

When Sherman had once seen Hood well on his way towards the North he knew that he had the whole Confederacy to pick from, excepting only that part of Virginia which was guarded by Lee. His own army consisted of sixty thousand tried and experienced men, and he understood perfectly how impossible it would then be to get together any fresh body of Southern troops that could withstand him for an hour. The course he decided upon in this situation of affairs was to march across Georgia to the sea, capture Savannah, and then turn and make his way to Virginia so as to help Grant finish his work at Richmond. As he was in a region which had not yet been ravaged by war, and which could therefore readily furnish the necessary supplies for the support of his army on its march, he destroyed all railroads and telegraphic communications behind him so that neither friend nor foe could learn of his movements until he had carried out at least part of his plans. Nearly a month was occupied in reaching Savannah, no resistance being offered to his progress until, towards

GEORGE H. THOMAS.

the end of his journey, he arrived at Fort McAllister, erected near the mouth of the Savannah River for the defence of the city. This was easily overcome in a fifteen minutes' attack and Savannah itself soon followed after a siege of only a week (Dec. 21), in ample time for Sherman to send the good news as "a Christmas present" to Lincoln. This closed Sherman's campaign for 1864. It was already near the end of the year, and before making any further move it was really necessary to give his men the rest which their long march had so richly earned for them. Accordingly Sherman did not again take the field until 1865 had opened.

Though Savannah was the only port captured by the North in 1864, attempts were made upon two of the other three which were still in possession of the Confederates. The attack on Mobile was so far successful as to effectually close it to blockade-runners. This was accomplished by Farragut's capturing the two forts which guarded it (August), after first defeating and taking the "Tennessee," an ironclad ram which with some gunboats had been stationed in Mobile Bay to aid the forts in defending the city. The other seaport which was attempted was Wilmington, and the expedition against it was jointly conducted by General But-

DAVID GLASCOE FARRAGUT.

ler and Admiral Porter (December); but they found Fort Fisher, by which it was protected, too strong for them. Both of these places (Mobile and Wilmington), however, fell into federal hands shortly after the beginning of the new year.

Besides the "Tennessee" the South lost another ironclad during 1864. This was the "Albemarle," which had been very active that year on the North Carolina coast, interfering greatly with Union operations in that State. It was destroyed one dark night in October by a small naval party under the leadership of Lieutenant Cushing, who at the risk of their own lives blew it up with a torpedo. The Confederates also lost that same year their three principal privateers, the "Alabama," the "Florida" and the "Georgia," all British built and armed, and manned chiefly by Englishmen. These had done much injury to the commerce of the United States, and though others soon took their place the disappearance of these three from the high seas was a cause of congratulation at the time to the North. The British origin of these privateers and the half sort of protection they received in English waters aroused considerable resentment against the government of Great Britain, which outlasted the war and was not ended until England, as will be seen later on, made good part of the damage they had done to American commerce,

ADMIRAL DAVID D. PORTER.

CHAPTER XXVIII.

THE RETURN OF PEACE.

ON February 1, 1865, Sherman left Savannah and started north towards Virginia. He had nearly reached Goldsboro in North Carolina when he was confronted by his old enemy, Johnston, who had been summoned from his retirement and who had hastily got together an army of forty thousand men to try to stem the federal advance. This army was made up principally of the garrisons of such seaboard towns as still belonged to the Confederates and which, left thus defenceless by the departure of those who had been protecting them, now quickly fell into Northern hands. Johnston threw his whole force against Sherman (March 19) in so sharp an attack that at first the chances seemed in favor of his winning the victory, but Sherman finally beat him off and entered Goldsboro. There the Union army paused to await the arrival of more troops, and during that pause the conquest of Richmond was completed.

Grant had been steadily at work strengthening and extending his line about Petersburg and Richmond, keeping Lee no less busy in guarding the defences of those cities. But as Grant's line crept slowly around, Lee found it harder and harder with his smaller army to properly oppose it. When therefore, early in March, Sheridan brought his cavalry up from the Shenandoah valley to assist Grant by operating on the western side of Richmond, Lee was unable to offer any adequate resistance, and Sheridan, by destroying the railroad, canal and bridges between Lynchburg and the Confederate capital, was able to still further reduce the supplies of Lee and so embarrass him yet more seriously. Sheridan then joined Grant, who thereupon pushed

THE HOUSE WHERE GENERAL LEE SURRENDERED.

his line another step to the west. Lee met it, but to do so he had to again weaken his force, which was already weak enough, and this last drain upon it proved a disastrous one. In the game which these two great commanders were playing the superior numbers of Grant were bound to count. He had now one hundred thousand men to Lee's fifty thousand, the latter drawn out in a thin line to defend the fortifications which Grant was hourly threatening.

overtook him, and on April 9, at a little place on the Lynchburg road called Appomattox Court House, Lee tendered his sword to Grant. Seventeen days later Johnston made a similar surrender to Sherman at Raleigh and in the course of the few following weeks the rest of the Confederacy had laid down its arms and the four years' struggle was over. The United States had ceased to be a divided nation and the whole country was one again.

While the North was still celebrating the fall of

THE SURRENDER OF GENERAL LEE.

The time for the final move had at last come. Grant advanced his entire army against Lee's entrenchments, attacking them simultaneously at every point (April 2). Such a united assault the Confederates were powerless to withstand, and their line broke and gave way. Seeing the hopelessness of any further effort to save the city he had so long shielded, Lee drew off his army in the night towards the west, and on April 3 the Union flag was again raised over Richmond. Lee did not retreat far. Grant had at once hastened after him and soon

Richmond and the surrender of Lee, and before the opportunity was given it to add Johnston's submission to its jubilation, its rejoicing was suddenly stopped and in an instant turned into mourning by news of the murder of Lincoln. The martyr President, who had safely led his people through the perils and horrors of civil war, had but barely entered upon a second term of office, to which he had been elected by an overwhelming majority of the people, when his life was cut short by the bullet of an assassin. His death was the result of a conspiracy formed by a number of persons in Washington and its vicinity, who thought that by killing the leading members of the administration the federal government would be thrown into a confusion that might give the Confederacy another hope of prolonging its existence. The head of the conspiracy was an actor, J. Wilkes Booth, and he it was who shot Lincoln in the presence of the audience of a

No Confederate leader, it is believed, was in any way connected with this crime.

The tragic end of Lincoln's life gave an emphasis to his virtues and to the services he had rendered his countrymen during the period of their great trial such as perhaps nothing else would have done. No other of our great Presidents had had so few natural advantages in their youth to help fit them for

RICHMOND, THE CONFEDERATE CAPITAL, ENTERED BY THE UNION ARMY.

public theatre in Washington on the evening of April 14, 1865. Lincoln lived but a few hours, dying early on the following day. Fortunately his was the only life lost. The misfortune was that the one life sacrificed should have chanced to be his. The conspiracy, with this great exception, miserably failed. The only other person injured was the Secretary of State, William H. Seward, who was slightly wounded but who fully recovered. Booth was pursued and in the pursuit was shot and killed; four of his associates were hung and four of them sent to prison.

the high office they were afterwards chosen to fill. Not one of them began his duties amid so many difficulties and perplexities. With unwavering patience and industry, with never-failing charity and tenderness, with profound sagacity and wisdom, he unravelled the tangle before him, united the many different factions of the North, touched and held the hearts of the people, carried them with him and was borne up by them through the dark days of the great war. We can conceive of no American excepting the great Washington who could for a single hour have taken the place or done the work of Abraham Lincoln.

The death of Lincoln raised to the presidency for the third time the Vice-President. Up to the outbreak of the Civil War, Andrew Johnson, the new President, had been a Democrat. He had been born in North Carolina, but before reaching manhood had removed to Tennessee. That State, in addition to making him her Governor, had sent him to Congress as a Representative for ten years and as a Senator for five years. Though he was a Southern Democrat he was a Unionist and was the only Senator who refused to follow his State when it seceded. He had done good service during the war as Military Governor of Tennessee, and it was in appreciation of this and of his exceptional loyalty, as well as in recognition of the support given the federal government by other war Democrats, that the Republicans had placed his name with Lincoln's on their ticket in 1864. Their opponents at that election were General McClellan and George H. Pendleton, nominated on a Democratic platform which declared the war to be a failure and that it ought to be stopped. In this the North did not agree with them and they received very few votes. The seceding States of course took no part in that election.

The total number of men who were engaged in the war was about four millions, two-thirds on the Northern side and one-third on the Southern. The number of lives lost was in the neighborhood of six hundred thousand, pretty evenly divided between the two parties in the struggle. Of these less than one-half were killed in battle or died from

WILLIAM HENRY SEWARD.

wounds received in battle. The others were carried off by camp diseases (which are always more fruitful sources of death in warfare than sword or gun) or else died in prison. These were the direct losses. But undoubtedly many others have since passed away whose friends could trace the beginning of impaired health to the exposures and sufferings undergone on the march or in the trench.

The United States government paid out nearly eight hundred millions of dollars during the course of the war and owed at its close nearly three thousand millions more. In addition to this the Northern States, cities and towns spent money freely in raising, equipping and transporting troops, and many individuals contributed largely from their private means in providing comforts for the soldiers on the field or in the hospital. How much was spent by the Confederate government or people is not known, and we cannot even guess, with any approach to accuracy, at the value of the property destroyed during the struggle. All that we do know is that the total cost of the war in one way or another to the country at large was simply enormous. But vast as this expenditure was there are few Americans to-day who would hesitate in

LINCOLN MONUMENT, SPRINGFIELD, ILLINOIS.

saying that lives and money were both well spent in preserving the Union; and there are probably now as many men in the South as in the North who are heartily glad that the failure of secession involved the extinction of slavery.

Before the conflict was decided and while the war was still in progress, the number of States was enlarged by the admission of West Virginia and Nevada. The first of these had formed the northwestern part of Virginia and was a mountainous region, which had been settled principally by emigrants from Ohio and in which there was little slave-holding. It had opposed the secession movement and had refused to be bound by the ordinance when that was adopted by the rest of Virginia, but had remained loyal to the Union and had set up a State government of its own. This Congress soon recognized by giving it (in 1863) the full privileges of statehood. Nevada had been a portion of the territory ceded with California by Mexico in 1848. The discovery of its silver mines in 1858 had attracted many people there, and this induced Congress in 1864 to make of it a State. Its importance lies almost entirely in its great mineral wealth, as its soil is too dry for agriculture. Its growth has been slow and its population since its admission has remained the smallest of any of the States.

CHAPTER XXIX.

RECONSTRUCTION OF THE SOUTH.

AFTER a review before their commanders and the officers of the government in Washington which lasted two days, the armies of the United States in the summer of 1865 were disbanded and the men went back to their homes to resume the occupations which they had laid aside when they took up arms. Fifty thousand of them, however, were retained for a while longer in service to preserve order in the Southern States, which were naturally in a very disturbed condition resulting from their having so long been the scene of war. As soon as the discharge of the soldiers had been seen to, the President and Congress were at liberty to devote themselves to the many other matters which were pressing upon their attention for early settlement.

Among the most important questions thus to be considered and determined were those in regard to the national debt, the rights of the freedmen (or negroes who had formerly been slaves) and the government of the States which had seceded. The first of these was settled with the least difficulty. It was decided to pay off the debt as rapidly as possible by continuing the high taxes established during the war and which, now that there were no war expenses, would yield a revenue much more than sufficient for the ordinary needs of government, and by applying the surplus to diminishing the debt. This has steadily been done until now (1889) nearly two-thirds of the great sum of money borrowed by the United States has been repaid to those who loaned it.

The other two matters were closely connected together and were not so easily arranged. The problems to be solved were how to protect the negroes in the enjoyment of the freedom that had been given to them and how to restore to the Southern States their share in the government of the country without again putting in peril all that the North had been contending for. The North had been fighting to keep the South in the Union and it had succeeded. It was content with this and had no wish, now that the war was over, to punish any one connected with it. When Lee and Johnston surrendered they were not put under arrest, but were allowed to return with their men to their homes on simply giving their word that they would fight no more. Other officers and soldiers were treated with equal generosity. No member of the Confederate Cabinet was taken to task for his part in bringing about the rebellion. Even the head and chief originator of the secession, Jefferson Davis, though he was detained for a time at Fortress Monroe, was soon released and has since remained at perfect liberty. No person was punished for treason; no one was even tried for it. Every one, high or low, and without regard to his share in the rebellion, has had the same freedom of action since the war closed as he had when it began.

But while the North had no revenge to gratify and no disposition to exact penalties from those it had defeated, it did not propose to lose the benefits of the victories it had won by readmitting the Confederates to all their political privileges without any pledges from them. Some guarantees were required that the South would accept the issues settled by the war and not try to reopen them. This was felt to be particularly necessary for the sake of the negroes. The South had wished to keep them slaves and naturally would not regard with much favor their present condition of freedom, and it was feared that, if left to themselves, some of the Southern States might seek to reduce them again to bondage or to something at least very nearly like it.

On this subject President Johnson and Congress held decidedly different opinions. Though he was a strong Union man, the President was a Southerner and did not care much about the freedmen, but he was an earnest believer in State rights. His theory was that the Southern States had never been out of the Union because they had not been allowed to leave it, and that their (white) citizens had the same right to vote, hold office and exercise their other political powers now that they had always had. He was therefore an advocate of allowing the Confederates to at once resume their full share in the government without imposing any conditions upon them. In accordance with these ideas he, immediately after taking office, appointed provisional governors of the Southern States who called conventions composed only of white men to reorganize their State governments. These conventions repealed the ordinances of secession which had been adopted in 1860 and 1861; ratified the Thirteenth Amendment to the Constitution which abolished slavery (and which the Northern States had accepted earlier in the same year); and agreed never to pay any debt which had been contracted in aiding the Confederacy. On this basis all of the Southern States became reorganized during 1865.

Congress did not dispute that the Southern States were still in the Union; on that point it agreed with Johnson. What it did claim was that the Confederates had voluntarily given up all their political rights when they rebelled, and that these rights must be restored to them before they could again use them. And Congress was determined not to restore these rights until it was satisfied that the freedmen would receive ample protection.

This resolve was strengthened by the course pursued by the Southern States after their reconstruction on Johnson's plan. Fearing that the ex-slaves would not work now that they had no one to compel them to, and that they would become a burden for the white people to support, these States enacted laws condemning all idle negroes to prison and to hard labor. The North considered this as something but little better than slavery under another name and it refused to recognize the State governments which had been thus formed with the President's approval, and the Senators and Representatives

ANDREW JOHNSON.

whom they sent to Washington were denied admittance by the Republican majority in control of Congress.

Congress wished to secure permanently for the negroes the privilege of voting, and it wished to withhold this privilege from the Confederates, or at least from the prominent ones. In this way, and this way only, it thought, could the freedmen defend themselves from oppression by their former masters. With the ballot in their hands they could control legislation and so look after their own interests. The political power of the South would be transferred from the disloyal whites to the loyal blacks, who would be in sympathy with their Republican friends of the North, and all danger would be removed of any further difficulties between the two races or between the two sections of the country. It was some time before Congress could mature a plan for best carrying this idea into effect, but it finally did so early in 1867. Johnson vigorously opposed the measure, but the Republicans were able to pass it over his veto by the two-thirds majority in each branch of Congress required by the Constitution.

The plan of Congress provided for the formation of entirely new State governments in the South and the adoption of another Amendment to the Constitution. This Amendment (which made the Fourteenth) gave the right to vote to all negroes and took it away from all Confederates who had held any important position in the United States army or navy, in the federal government or in their States before the war. Congress, however, was given power to restore their political rights to those now deprived of them whenever it should see fit to do so by a two-thirds vote. The Amendment also pledged the people that the national debt should be paid in full and that no part of the Confederate debt should ever be acknowledged or redeemed. If the Southern States ratified this Amendment and organized governments satisfactory to Congress, then Congress would recognize them and admit their Senators and Representatives. But these governments must be formed by conventions in whose selection all freedmen (and no prominent Confederates) should have a voice. To insure this the President was authorized to appoint military governors, who were to supervise the election of the delegates and see that the negroes had the opportunity of voting and that the Confederate leaders were prevented from doing so.

Southern whites did not much relish this plan, as they thought it placed the blacks who had once been their slaves too nearly in the position of now becoming their masters. But it was adopted, and in the course of 1867 and 1868 was accepted by all but four of the States lately in secession. The four exceptions were Virginia, Texas, Mississippi and Georgia, which all stood out against it until 1870 and were therefore without representation in Congress during this period. One State, Tennessee, had not waited for this action of Congress before remodelling her government in accordance with Northern ideas, and she had been readmitted in 1866, while Congress was still engaged in considering a scheme for the admission of the others.

The result of the Fourteenth Amendment and of the legislation which accompanied it was to give the control of affairs in the South to a body of very ignorant and very inexperienced voters. That they would not use their power very wisely at first might have been expected, and the condition of the Southern States for a number of years after the war was anything but prosperous. Matters, however, have since then gradually, if slowly, improved. The negroes have learned that freedom does not mean idleness and that they have only their own labor to depend upon for their support. More of them are becoming educated and all of them are becoming more industrious. From time to time Congress has removed their disabilities from the Confederates and now Jefferson Davis remains the only one who cannot exercise all the political privileges he once enjoyed, and without doubt they would also be restored to him should he apply for them. The Confederates who have thus been received back into citizenship were those best qualified to lead in the arts of peace as well as in the arts of war, and under their guidance their part of the country has developed in many directions and with a rapidity unknown in its earlier history. But before this new era of prosperity began in the South it suffered much from poverty and the ignorantly framed laws enacted by the freedmen in their first days of power.

The disagreement between Johnson and Congress regarding the treatment of the South soon extended to other questions and constantly grew more bitter. Each viewed every act of the other with hostility and suspicion. The President attempted to thwart the will of Congress by vetoing (or refusing to approve or sign) bills which it passed, but this was of little benefit to him and of little harm to the Republicans, as their two-thirds majority in each house enabled them to dispense with his signature to any measure upon which they were united and which they really cared should become a law. One of these bills was the "tenure-of-office" act, prohibiting the President from removing any high official in the government service unless the Senate consented. This became a law in the same month that the reconstruction act was passed, March, 1867. Johnson refused to obey it on the ground that the Constitution had given the President the right of removal and that Congress had no power to take the right away. Accordingly not long afterwards he dismissed Edwin M. Stanton, who had been the Secretary of War since the beginning of Lincoln's administration. For this, as well as for some other acts which it considered contrary to law, the House of Representatives resolved to impeach him.

RECONSTRUCTION OF THE SOUTH.

The Constitution makes it the duty of the lower branch of Congress, when it believes that any important member of the government has disobeyed the law or been unfaithful to his trust, to accuse him of his offences before the Senate, which then regularly tries him very much as other offenders are tried in courts. This is called impeachment. Johnson is the only President of the United States who

with political troubles. It gave attention as well to foreign affairs. Among these was a difficulty not with, but in, Mexico.

Taking advantage of the disturbances in the United States caused by the Civil War, France in the early part of that struggle had sent an army into Mexico, overthrown its republican government, converted it into a monarchy and placed the Arch-

EDWIN M. STANTON.

has been impeached, though one or two other officials, less eminent than a President, have been. In the case of Johnson the proceedings lasted nearly four months (from February to May, 1868) and resulted in his acquittal, as not quite two-thirds of the Senators were convinced of his guilt. A change of a single vote, however, would have deposed him from his office.

But this administration was not entirely occupied

duke Maximilian on the throne. Our government had strongly protested against this as a violation of the principles of the Monroe doctrine, but it was then too busily engaged in fighting its own battles to back up its protest with armed force. France had paid no heed to our objections. She believed, as did also Great Britain at the time, that the rebellion was on too large a scale to be suppressed; that the Confederacy would succeed in establishing itself; that the Union would be permanently broken up; and that, when it had become divided and the war was ended, neither fragment would be able, even if it should care, to interfere with her. She therefore kept her soldiers in Mexico to uphold Maximilian in his efforts to rule that country against the will of its people.

Events did not turn out exactly as France had anticipated. She found that the federal government had the strength to stop secession and crush rebellion, and so, when the war was over, she became much more ready to listen to arguments on the application of the Monroe doctrine than she had been in 1863, and on our renewed demand in 1867 she recalled her troops to France. At his own desire Maximilian was left behind to see if he could govern without the aid of foreign bayonets. The United States had no objections to make to this. If the Mexicans desired him for their emperor they were welcome to him, as long as no European power attempted to compel them to retain him. But they did not want him. As soon as his French protectors were gone, he was attacked, defeated, captured and shot, and Mexico again became a republic.

Another foreign matter and one of a pleasanter character was also arranged at this time. This was the purchase from Russia in 1867 of Alaska for seven millions and two hundred thousand dollars. Alaska is the last of the accessions made to the territory of the United States and increased its area nearly six hundred thousand square miles. The size of our country is now more than four times what it was at the close of the Revolutionary War. It was then about eight hundred thousand square miles. The Louisiana cession added a little over a million,

Florida about sixty thousand, Texas nearly four hundred thousand and the Mexican grant not quite five hundred and fifty thousand, so that the total number of square miles now included within it is a trifle over three millions and six hundred thousand.

During the same year that Alaska was bought and Maximilian put to death the thirty-seventh State entered the Union. Nebraska, like so many of the other Western States, had been part of the Louisiana purchase and had been organized into a Territory by itself at the time of the heated anti-slavery contest for the possession of Kansas (1854). Its growth, however, had not been nearly as rapid as was that of its sister Territory, as it had been explored but little and no one then even suspected that the fertility and richness of its soil would soon make it one of the most productive of the American States.

The last, but by no means the least important, event to be noted in this period is the connecting of Europe with America by telegraph. Efforts to accomplish this had been tried many times before but they had all failed. In 1857 a telegraphic cable was drawn across the bottom of the Atlantic which at first, it was thought, would prove a success. But it did not work satisfactorily, nor did the others that followed it until in 1866 the difficulties were overcome and one was laid which has operated as perfectly as its predecessors on land had done. This has since then been supplemented by others, and there are now a number of lines between the two continents, so that quick international communication is not subject to the risk of accident to any one wire. The commercial and political benefit that this extension of Morse's invention has been to both countries it is hardly necessary to point out.

CHAPTER XXX.

THE PRESIDENCY OF GENERAL GRANT.

JOHNSON's quarrel with Congress brought him great unpopularity and when his term drew towards a close he did not obtain even a nomination for continuance in office. On March 4, 1869, he was succeeded in the presidency by General Grant, whom the Republicans easily elected over the Democratic candidate, Horatio Seymour, who had lately been Governor of New York.

A native of Ohio, Grant received at his birth the name of Hiram Ulysses, but by a mistake he was entered as Ulysses S. when he began his military career as a cadet at West Point, and he found it so difficult afterwards to have this official record altered that he was constrained to use for the rest of his life a name thus thrust upon him by accident. He remained in the army for a few years after graduating from West Point, rising to the position of Captain during the course of the Mexican war, and then resigned his commission to enter into business. When the Civil War began he was living

THE PRESIDENCY OF GENERAL GRANT.

in Illinois and he at once offered his services to the government. They were accepted and from the start he met with almost unbroken success and steadily rose in rank from that of Colonel to that of General, the latter title being one which Washington alone had borne before and which has since been bestowed upon only two others, Sherman and Sheridan.

Two months after the inauguration of Grant the Central Pacific Railroad, connecting California with the East, and which had been building since 1862, was completed and thrown open to the public. This was an event of hardly less value than the laying of the Atlantic cable a year or two previous had been. It brought San Francisco and New York nearer together than Boston and Washington had been sixty years before and has been of the same helpfulness in the development of the extreme West that the first steamboats and railroads were in settling the Mississippi region in the early part of the century. Other Pacific roads have since been built, north and south of the first one, so

the country during the first few years following the war. It was a prosperity in which nearly every one, at least in the North and West, had a share. Crop failures in Europe gave a good market to our agri-

HORATIO SEYMOUR.

cultural products. The heavy taxation retained for the purpose of reducing the national debt stimulated manufactures. Gold and silver mines yielded

ON THE CENTRAL PACIFIC RAILROAD.

that there are now ample means of communication between the two oceans.

The completion of the Central Pacific was only one sign of a general prosperity which spread over

a large quantity of the precious metals. Immigration, which had fallen off during the war, became greater than ever and helped to people the interior of the continent with a class of settlers who in the main not only knew how to work but who were only too glad to use the opportunities for well-paid labor offered them by the great republic.

What Grant's administration will probably always be most closely associated with is the substitution for the first time in history of arbitration in the place of war as a means of settling a serious difference between nations. The United States had a grievance against Great Britain for the sympathy shown by the latter with the Confederates in the opening years of the rebellion. With few exceptions the ruling classes in England and their leaders hoped and believed that the North would be defeated and the Union divided, and they had little hesitancy in freely saying so. Had this sympathy been limited to words, our government would have had no ground for formal complaint, however keenly it felt the want of friendliness thus displayed. But the sympathy extended beyond words. For though no open aid was given to the Confederates they were permitted to purchase vessels in Great Britain, and arm and equip them in English harbors for privateer service, and this we claimed was a violation of the law of nations and rendered the British government liable for the damage inflicted by these vessels upon American commerce.

England was not disposed to admit the claim and the question was discussed by the two countries for a number of years before any agreement could be reached. Then a treaty was signed at Washington in 1871 which provided among other things that this matter should be submitted to five judges and each side bound itself to abide by their decision. These judges or arbitrators were to be appointed one each by the Emperor of Brazil, the President of the Swiss Confederation, the King of Italy, the Queen of England and the President of the United States. They met at Geneva in 1872 and the whole subject was carefully considered, the facts in the case examined and established and the views of each party in the controversy argued at length before them. The conclusion they arrived at was favorable to the American government and fifteen and a half millions of dollars was fixed upon as the amount of the damage that the United States were justly entitled to, and this sum was accordingly paid over to us by Great Britain.

It ought to be said in this connection, however, that sympathy with the South was by no means universal in England. While nearly all of those who governed the country were arrayed on the side of the slave-owners, the great body of the common people, the middle classes and the workingmen, believed heartily that the North was in the right and that it must and would win in the stupendous struggle that was convulsing the country; and they did not suffer themselves to be moved from this belief or to be stirred from the side of free labor for which the Unionists were fighting, though they had almost the strongest reason that men can ever have for wishing that the war was over or that it had never been begun. For to many of them the war meant starvation. It shut out the raw cotton from Great Britain. This compelled the mills in which the cotton was manufactured to close. The closing of the factories threw their hands out of work, and want of work was want of food. But their own sufferings did not deter them from advocating the cause of the North and remaining its true and loyal friends, and it was their influence, voiced by only a few leaders, like John Bright, Thomas Hughes and Richard Cobden, which had held back the English government from publicly recognizing the Confederacy as an independent nation.

The Washington treaty not only disposed of the "Alabama" claims but it also settled the last boundary dispute which has arisen between the two countries, that affecting the extreme northwestern point of the United States (between Vancouver's Island and the State of Washington). This was also decided in our favor. But we did not fare so well in the third matter arranged by this same treaty, which had relation to the damages due Great Britain for American fishing in Canadian waters. As in the "Alabama" claims, the determination of the question was left to arbitrators and they awarded the English government five and a half millions of dollars.

Before the treaty of Washington was signed another Amendment to the Constitution was proposed and ratified by the people (1870). It forbids any State to deprive a citizen of the privilege of voting or of any other right on account of " his race, color or previous condition of servitude," and was intended to make still more secure the freedom and liberty of the negroes. It is the last Constitutional Amendment which has been adopted and is numbered the fifteenth.

Grant's administration lasted for eight years, but the prosperity which marked its opening did not continue with it till the end. In 1871 there was a great fire in Chicago, followed in 1872 by one nearly as disastrous in Boston, in each of which a large part of the city was burnt and many millions of dollars' worth of property destroyed. The next year (1873) a financial panic occurred which produced great distress and a business depression of which the effect was felt for some years. This was attributed to several causes, the principal one being the same as that which led to the panic in 1857, too rapid railroad building in the West. But there were other reasons for it as well, excessive speculation, overproduction of manufactures and the inflated prices for goods of all kinds which had been maintained since the war. The panic was really a reaction against these prices and resulted in very much lessening them.

In addition to these commercial and industrial misfortunes there arose also considerable political discontent. General Grant's appointments to office were not always thought to be very wise ones even by members of his own party. A number of cases of dishonesty in prominent officials were discovered before his first term ended, and created a feeling of dissatisfaction in many Republicans. Others among those who had once been his adherents disapproved of the policy of employing federal troops any longer in the South for the protection of the negroes. They held that even if the negroes were ill-treated

were the Northern States. When, therefore, the Republicans renominated General Grant in 1872, a section of the party, calling themselves Liberal Republicans, named Horace Greeley, the editor of the New York *Tribune,* for the presidency and the Democrats accepted him also as their candidate.

TRIBUNE BUILDING, NEW YORK CITY.

The movement, however, was a failure and General Grant was given another term.

His second term witnessed the beginning of a series of centennial celebrations of Revolutionary battles and of events connected with the gaining of our independence and the organizing of our government which have been continued through the administrations of the four Presidents who have followed him. Beginning with the one hundredth anniversary of the fight at Lexington on April 19, 1875, the successive steps in the struggle of the young nation towards freedom and unity have been recalled and fitly honored and commemorated. Bunker Hill, Saratoga and Yorktown, as each came round, were gratefully remembered and observed; but the two celebrations into which the whole people have most heartily entered have been those which marked the throwing aside of the English rule and the adoption in its stead of the Constitutional one. On July 4, 1876, the centennial of the Declaration of Independence was greeted with rejoicing in every village, town and city throughout the land; on April 30, 1889, the one hundredth

HORACE GREELEY.

and prevented from voting, as in some cases they undoubtedly were, it was the duty of the State and not of the national government to correct such evils; and that the Southern States, having been reconstructed and readmitted, should now be left to themselves and treated in all respects exactly as

anniversary of the inauguration of Washington as the first President of the United States was made a special national holiday that every one might have an opportunity of showing in some way his appreciation of the blessings which a century of union and freedom had brought to the people. In New York particularly was this latter day made one of great festivity and splendid display, as it was in that city that the federal government had begun its existence.

Besides the processions, orations and monuments with which these centennial anniversaries were marked, an exposition was held at Philadelphia in 1876, to which all the world was invited to contribute examples of their products and manufactures that an opportunity might be afforded of comparing the progress made in our short history with that of other nations and of displaying the wonderful resources of this country. The exposition was open for six months and during that period the large buildings erected for the purpose were daily thronged with great crowds gathered from every quarter of the globe who had come to examine the myriad objects on exhibition.

Shortly before Grant retired from office the thirty-eighth State was admitted to the Union (1876). Colorado takes its name from the principal river flowing through its western territory, and was formed by uniting a portion of the old Louisiana tract to part of the Mexican grant. Its gold and silver mines led to its first settlement, and its wealth thus far has been derived chiefly from its mineral resources. Of late, however, the raising of cattle for market has become an important industry in Colorado, for which it is excellently adapted as much of its land is better adapted for grazing than for any other purpose.

CHAPTER XXXI.

MR. HAYES'S ADMINISTRATION.

THE most closely contested election in American history was that for Grant's successor. The opposing candidates were R. B. Hayes on the Republican side and S. J. Tilden on the Democratic. There was no one question dividing the people at the time, as slavery or the tariff had on other occasions; the platforms of the two parties were pretty much the same; and the struggle between them was simply one for possession of the government. Their strength was very nearly equal. The Republicans had lost the large majorities with which a few years before they had carried every election, most of the war Democrats who for a while had acted with them having returned to their former allegiance, and a number of moderate Republicans having also left their party on account of the scandals connected with Grant's administration and its policy in the South. The Democrats had regained control of nearly all of the Southern States and of some of the Northern ones as well. In 1874 they secured the lower branch of Congress. When 1876 arrived they were in an excellent position, they thought, to once more obtain the presidency.

When the election was over it was found that each candidate had received nearly the same number of votes and for quite a time the result was in a great deal of doubt. Both sides claimed to have carried certain Southern States, and the votes of these States were necessary to give either Mr. Hayes or Mr. Tilden a majority. Congress was not able to decide the question, as neither the Republican Senate nor Democratic House would

RUTHERFORD B. HAYES.

consent to awarding the presidency to its political opponent. After many plans for solving the difficulty had been suggested and thrown aside, the leaders of the two parties agreed to submit the disputed votes to a special tribunal to be created for the purpose. This tribunal or court was named the "Electoral Commission" and was composed of five Senators, five Representatives and five judges of the Supreme Court. The various points at issue about the election were laid before it and by a vote of eight to seven were determined in favor of Mr. Hayes, who accordingly in 1877 became the nineteenth President of the United States.

Rutherford B. Hayes was a native and resident of Ohio and served with distinction through the entire course of the Civil War. At its close he entered the lower branch of Congress and after remaining there for one term (two years) was chosen governor of his State. To this position he was subsequently twice reëlected, and it was to the popularity he gained as Ohio's chief magistrate that he owed his presidential nomination by the Republicans.

Almost his first act on taking office was to withdraw the federal troops from the Southern States, thus placing them on the same footing as was the North. He had promised this in his inaugural address and he lost no time in making good his word. Though this did not remove the last trace of the war, it destroyed the last outward sign of Southern subjection to the North, and it greatly helped to restore a cordial feeling between the two sections. The two parts of the country have steadily drawn nearer together since that day and are now united by a much stronger bond than at any other time in their history since the beginning of the great anti-slavery controversy nearly seventy years ago.

With one exception the administration of President Hayes was a very peaceful one. The exception occurred during the first year of his term, in the summer of 1877, and was occasioned by a general lowering of the wages of railroad employés throughout the country. The men resisted this reduction, left the employment of the railroad companies and attempted to prevent others from taking their places and trains from being run. This caused disturbances and riots in several States, the most serious ones breaking out in Pennsylvania, particularly at Pittsburg. Order was not restored until the aid of State militia, in some instances also of United States soldiers, had been obtained, and before this was done some millions of dollars' worth of property had been destroyed and a hundred and fifty or more lives lost.

In national politics the matters of most interest in this period are connected with finance: silver was made a legal tender, a large part of the public debt was refunded, and specie payments were resumed. When the government was suddenly called upon in 1861 and 1862 to meet the great expenses of the war, it did so partly by increasing the taxes, partly by borrowing money for which it gave its bonds, and partly by issuing paper money with which it paid some of its expenses instead of with gold. This paper money was issued in large quantities both by the government and by national banks established under authority of the government. As the paper money was only a promise to pay a certain amount of gold at some indefinite time in the future, it was of course of less value than the gold itself, and it quickly drove gold out of circulation.

SAMUEL J. TILDEN.

From 1862 to 1879 specie (or coin) payments were suspended and the money affairs of the nation were conducted with paper currency. By 1879 the government found itself in a prosperous enough condition again to fulfil its promises, and accordingly it then announced itself prepared to redeem with coin all the paper money presented at the national treasury for payment, and holders of government notes or of bank bills have since that year been able at any time to exchange them for gold.

The uniform promptness with which the government had paid the interest on its bonds and the unprecedented rapidity with which it had been reducing the debt gave it excellent credit and it became able to borrow money on much better terms than in the days of the war. President Hayes's Secretary of the Treasury, John Sherman, took advantage of this favorable condition to exchange the older bonds as they became due for new ones bearing a lower rate of interest, and in this way the country has been yearly saved a considerable sum of money. Mr. Sherman's successors have continued his policy, and the national debt (that part of it, at least, which is still unpaid) has now been all refunded, much of it at a rate of interest less than one-half of what was paid for the first war loan.

The resumption of specie payments and the refunding of the public debt were both acts of which the President heartily approved. But the third financial measure of his administration was adopted by Congress against his judgment and over his veto. Silver dollars had originally been lawful money (or a *legal tender* for the payment of any debt) as well as gold. There had not been many of them coined, however, and they had not been very generally used, except in small quantities, until after the American mines had begun to add so enormously to the silver product of the world. Then the number of them greatly increased and their value naturally somewhat lessened, for any object as a rule grows less valuable as it becomes more plentiful or is more easily procured. But the value of silver not only decreased, it also fluctuated or varied as the yield of the mines each month was more or less. On account of this diminishing and unstable value as compared with that of gold, Congress, in 1873, following the example of many of the nations of Europe, demonetized the silver dollar, or took away its fixed legal tender character, so that it became simply an article of merchandise, to be bought or sold for the price it was really worth. After a five years' trial of gold as the only standard money, the people became dissatisfied with the change, as they thought the effect was chiefly to benefit the rich bondholders by securing to them the repayment of their loans to the government in gold, and Congress accordingly, in obedience to the wish of the people, in 1878, remonetized silver.

Since Morse thirty years before had shown that electricity could be employed in sending messages over a wire, many inventors had been engaged in trying to find other ways in which this wonderful agent could be used. And many had been found during these years; but the most remarkable of all was discovered and put into successful operation shortly after Mr. Hayes entered upon his presidency. The telephone is even a more curious invention than the telegraph, as it enables people to talk with each other at a considerable distance apart so that they hear the actual words uttered by the speaker and recognize the tones of his voice. At first only short distances of a few miles were attempted, but more recently it has been applied with satisfactory results at points separated by several hundred miles. If the telephone can be carried to the same degree of perfection that the telegraph has reached, it will rival the latter in value and usefulness, but it is doubtful if it can ever be made to cover as great a number of miles. In the meantime it has become one of the greatest of modern conveniences and in the cities and larger towns few business establishments of any size or importance are without telephonic instruments.

Lighting by electricity quickly followed talking by electricity, only a year separating the two discoveries (1877-78). The electric light has decided advantages over any means of illumination previously employed, as it not only affords a much stronger and clearer light, but in doing so it throws out no heat and does not affect the purity of the surrounding air. It is rapidly replacing gas in the streets of cities, in public buildings, and in many offices and mercantile houses, but its cost has thus far prevented its introduction into private dwellings except in a few occupied by the wealthier class.

A beginning was also made at this time in applying electricity as a substitute for steam-power in operating machinery and in drawing railroad cars. While some little progress has been made, it has not yet been developed to the same extent in this line that it has been in other directions. What other services this marvellous force of nature may do for man we cannot now even imagine; but we may feel certain that there remain undiscovered innumerable ways in which this invisible power will be made to minister to our needs and comforts.

CHAPTER XXXII.

THE CIVIL SERVICE AND THE MORMONS.

ON his retiring from office in 1877 General Grant had set out on a tour around the world, during which he had been received with the highest honors and distinction by the people and rulers of the many countries he had visited on his travels. From this

GENERAL W. S. HANCOCK.

journey he had but lately returned when in 1880 Republican delegates met in convention at Chicago to choose their candidate to succeed Mr. Hayes, and a large and influential number of them made a strong effort to obtain the nomination for the great General. But since the day Washington had declined a third election it had been the unwritten law that no President should serve for more than eight years, and this traditional sentiment proved too powerful to be broken even in favor of the hero of Vicksburg, and the nomination went to General Garfield. In opposition to him the Democrats put forward General Winfield S. Hancock, the senior Major-General in the army and an officer who had won an enviable reputation at Gettysburg, Fredericksburg and on many another battlefield of the war. He had had no political experience, however, and his opponent had had, and so for this reason the latter was preferred by the people for the presidency.

James A. Garfield is a striking instance, of which Lincoln is the greatest but by no means the only other example, of a poor boy rising solely by his own exertions to the foremost place in our country. And it is the glory of America that such a chance is given to every lad, if he have the ability within him, to gain for himself whatever position he will, without let or hindrance from any one else. Indeed, Americans take the greatest pride in those from among themselves who have acquired their fame unaided by fortune or influence, but by the exercise of their own talents and through their own industry and perseverance.

Born in Ohio in the poorest circumstances and left fatherless while still an infant, Garfield's earliest years were spent in a hard struggle to obtain a livelihood. He was obliged to turn to whatever his hand found to do—working on a farm, chopping wood, driving horses on the tow-path of a canal. But in spite of the obstacles in his way he managed

JAMES A. GARFIELD.

to get time for study and to fit himself for college. After graduation he taught for a while and then began the practice of law, but he had hardly secured a start in that profession when the outbreak of the Civil War caused him to lay it aside to enter the army. There he had risen to the rank of Major-General, when in 1863 he was called from the field to Congress. For eighteen years he was continuously a member of the House of Representatives and had just been transferred to the Senate when another revolution of the wheel of fortune placed him in the White House.

His administration opened at another period of great prosperity to our country, for fortunately those periods in our history have been much more frequent than times of distress. The census taken in the year of his election disclosed a population of

CHESTER A. ARTHUR.

over fifty million people within the boundaries of the United States, an increase of more than eleven millions since the preceding count in 1870 was made. The effects of the financial crisis of 1873 had worn away, leaving business on a sounder and healthier basis than ever before. The Western railroads, whose building had helped bring about that panic, were now earning money for their owners by carrying supplies to the new settlements in the northern interior of the continent and by transporting the produce of that region to its ocean-market. Manufactories were all busy, giving profitable employment to thousands of hands. The tide of immigration was larger than ever and some of it now was turning towards the South. For the South was sharing in this prosperity as well as the West and North and was making more rapid strides in material advancement than one would have dreamed possible when Lee laid down his arms.

From the statesmanship he had displayed as a Congressman much was hoped from Garfield as a President, but unhappily no opportunity was given him to show how wise a ruler he could be. For the fourth time in their history the American people were called upon to lament the death of a President in office, and for the second time that death was by assassination. On July 2, 1881, as General Garfield was standing in a railroad station in Washington, he was shot by a disappointed office-seeker named Guiteau, and after suffering greatly for more than two months, died on September 19 at Elberon, N. J., where he had been removed in the hope that the cooler sea-air might benefit him. Until almost the very hour of his death it was thought that the wound might not prove fatal and that possibly he would recover. The patience with which he bore his sufferings upon his bed of pain heightened the admiration in which his character was already held by his countrymen and deepened their affectionate regard for him, and the day of his funeral was as generally observed as a day of mourning as that of Lincoln had been. The murderer was arrested almost in the very act of shooting, and after the death of his victim was tried, convicted and hung for the crime.

Chester A. Arthur, Garfield's Vice-President and successor, was indisputably the most able of the four men whom accident had placed in the presidential chair. He was born in Vermont, but most of his life was spent in New York in the practice of the profession of law. Though he had been prominent in political affairs for many years he had held no previous office excepting the collectorship of the port of New York (1871–1879), but he had rendered valuable aid during the war in raising, arming and transporting the quota of troops furnished to the Union armies by the State of his adoption. In politics he belonged to the "stalwart" wing of the Republican party which had advocated the renomination of Grant.

Garfield's death served to direct general attention to what had already been recognized by some few as a growing evil in the conduct of public business. Since Jackson's time every incoming President had been besieged by applicants for office, and the custom had become deeply rooted to change with each administration the great majority of office-holders. With the growth in population and settled territory the number of offices had of necessity also increased, so that there were now a much larger number of positions to be filled than in the earlier years of the government, and the pressure for appointment became correspondingly more severe. The result was in every way bad. Too much of the time of the Presidents and of prominent officials was consumed in considering the various claims presented for this or that place. Patronage became a power in deciding nominations and elections. Office-holders knew that they could better their chances of retention and promotion by zealous party work than by a diligent discharge of their regular duties. Public business was not performed with the same care that private business was, as there was not the same incentive to faithfulness in the one case that there was in the other. It suffered also from the constant replacement of experienced men by inexperienced ones, as well as from incompetent and negligent place-holders who secured a footing in the service through the favor of some influential party manager. All these and other objections to the four-yearly scramble for office had been felt by the few but not by the many, until Guiteau's miserable bullet forced them upon the mind of every one. That created a popular sentiment which demanded some remedy for these evils, and out of respect to that sentiment a law was enacted in 1883 providing for nonpartisan appointments to the lower grade of offices by competitive examinations. There has in consequence been some improvement since then in the civil service, but not nearly as much as the friends of the reform desire or hope in time to obtain.

Another reform was also attempted in this administration which, like that of the civil service, has been only partially successful. This was the suppression of polygamy among the Mormons in the Territory of Utah. The Mormons are a religious body founded in 1830 by a man named Joseph Smith, who claimed to be a prophet, and to have received a new revelation from God in the "Book of Mormon" discovered by him (he said) buried in the earth. Among the beliefs of these Mormons was that a man not only might but that he ought to have several wives—which is what the word "polygamy" means. The sect first established itself in Missouri, but public disfavor soon drove it out of that State. It then settled in Illinois, but there it was as roughly treated as in Missouri, and so (in 1844) it bought a large tract of land in Utah and removed thither.

THE MORMON TABERNACLE.

The United States government has many times endeavored to compel the Mormons to give up their objectionable marriage custom, but has never succeeded.

In 1882 Congress renewed the attempt by passing a much more severe law than any that had previously been enacted for the punishment of those convicted of polygamy. This law, it is thought, has checked the evil a little, but has by no means put an end to it. Were it not for polygamy, Utah would long ago have been given statehood, as its population is much greater than that of many of the States already in the Union.

CHAPTER XXXIII.

THE MOST RECENT EVENTS.

THOUGH Mr. Arthur's administration was generally considered a satisfactory one by his party and by the country, he failed to secure a nomination for a second term, the choice falling upon James G. Blaine,

JAMES G. BLAINE.

who had been Secretary of State during Garfield's few months of office and who, prior to that, had been United States Senator and Congressman from Maine. There was, however, on various grounds, a good deal of opposition to Mr. Blaine among the Republicans and as a consequence the Democratic candidate, Mr. Cleveland, was elected.

Grover Cleveland, the first Democrat to be chosen President since Buchanan (twenty-four years before) was replaced by Lincoln, had been in public life but a comparatively short time when he attained the presidency. The attention of his fellow-citizens had been first drawn to him by his excellent management of the affairs of Buffalo while Mayor of that city. This had induced the Democrats of New York to nominate him in 1882 for the governorship of that State. The enormous majority of one hundred and ninety-two thousand by which he was elected to this office at once gave him a foremost place as a popular leader and two years later earned for him the presidential nomination and succession.

His first executive act on entering upon his duties was to sign the commission restoring to General Grant the military rank which the latter had resigned on becoming President in 1869. The bill authorizing President Cleveland to do this was passed by Congress during the closing hours of Mr. Arthur's term, but out of courtesy to his successor Mr. Arthur left to Mr. Cleveland the privilege of issuing the commission. The country cordially approved of this renewed expression by its representatives of its appreciation and gratitude for Grant's services, but he did not long enjoy the honor which had thus a second time been conferred upon him, as on July 23, 1885, he died at Mount McGregor, N. Y., from an incurable cancer in the mouth.

Another act of Mr. Cleveland's which met with almost as much popular applause was his signature, just before he went out of office (1889), to a bill creating four more States, the largest number ever admitted to the Union at any one time. These were the States of Washington, Montana, North Dakota and South Dakota. The first of these had been under territorial government since 1853 and had been claimed (with Oregon and Idaho) as one of our possessions since the explorations made by Lewis and Clarke in 1804. Great Britain disputed the claim until 1846, when the question was adjusted by treaty. Its settlement was first stimulated by the discovery of gold in the California country and was rapidly hastened by the building of the Pacific railroads. The fertility of its soil is remarkable and it will undoubtedly soon become one of the richest of our agricultural States. The two Dakotas and Montana were all taken from the Louisiana purchase and had been organized as territories since 1861 and 1864 respectively, the Dakotas being under one government and undivided until their admission as States. Montana's wealth is chiefly in its mines; that of the Dakotas in their grain production. Washington and the Dakotas had been entitled from their population to statehood for a number of years before they received it, but Congressional disagreements kept it from them until the present time. The addition of these four stars to the American flag in the very year that marked the completion of the first century of the Constitution was considered by every one a most happy coincidence and afforded a further proof of the great expansion of our country during these hundred years—the original thirteen States having now grown to three and a half times that number.

The differences between Canada and the United States regarding the fisheries off the coast of the former country, which had been disposed of for a time by the Washington treaty of 1871, were revived during President Cleveland's administration and caused a little feeling between the people of the two nations. An effort was made to settle them by a fresh agreement drawn up by representatives appointed by England, the Dominion of Canada and our government, but the treaty which they drafted did not meet with the approval of the United States Senate (whose consent is needed to give effect to any treaty), and so the difficulties have not yet been removed. A temporary arrangement (called a *modus vivendi*), however, has been made by which any serious trouble is avoided until a permanent settlement of the matter can be effected by a treaty satisfactory to all the parties.

But neither the question of admitting the new States, on which the American people were practically agreed, nor the Canadian fishery dispute, on which they held decidedly different opinions, excited anything like the interest which was aroused by a renewal of the tariff discussion. The finances of the nation were at this time in a very peculiar condition. Owing to the rapid growth of the population and of the business of the country the revenue of the government had become very large and greatly in excess of all its needs. The surplus could no longer be applied, as it had been before, to the payment of bonds of the United States, because all the bonds that were due had been redeemed and the owners of the bonds which had not yet matured did not wish them paid, as they preferred that investment of their money to any other. In consequence of

GROVER CLEVELAND.

this the surplus revenue began to accumulate in the national treasury and the government found itself with more money on its hands than it knew what to do with, and the prospect of having still more from year to year. President Cleveland, thereupon, in a message sent to Congress when it met in December, 1887, recommended a reduction in the taxes, especially in the customs duties, so that the national income should not exceed the national expenditures and the surplus cease to grow any larger. The Democratic party adopted his views and prepared a bill giving effect to them. This the Republicans opposed from the protectionist standpoint that it would injure the manufacturing industries of the country. They proposed instead to increase the expenditures by more liberal pensions, by more generous appropriations for internal improvements, coast defences and naval vessels and by repaying to loyal States some of the money contributed by them for the prosecution of the war. They also proposed to slightly reduce the revenue by cutting down or abolishing altogether the few internal taxes still in force, and which are now chiefly limited to those levied on the manufacture of tobacco and malt and spirituous liquors. Though the schedule advocated by the Democrats would only have reduced the imports on an average a little more than five per cent., which they claimed would not injure American manufactures, it was the principle and not the amount of tariff reduction which the Republicans fought. The question was eagerly debated in Congress, in the newspapers, on the platform and by the people for a year, and became the principal issue at the presidential election in 1888. At that election Mr. Cleveland was renominated by the Democrats and General Harrison, a grandson of the ninth President, and a former Senator from Indiana, was put forward in opposition to him by the Republicans. The campaign was vigorously conducted by both sides and proved nearly as exciting a one as that of fifty years before when the elder Harrison was a candidate. The result was a victory for the Republicans, for though Mr. Cleveland's popular majority was larger than it had been in 1884, he failed, by a change in the votes of some States, to secure the electoral majority. Accordingly, on March 4, 1889, Benjamin Harrison became the twenty-third President of the United States.

In entering upon the second century of its existence the United States finds its people united, contented, and prosperous; at profound peace with all the world and looked up to and respected by every nation on the face of the globe. During its short period of life it has made far greater progress in every direction than was ever before made in the same

BENJAMIN HARRISON.

interval of time by any country since history began. The poor and the oppressed of every land have found within it a welcome and a home and a chance to make for themselves such a future as they could never have hoped to obtain in the place of their birth. Self-rule has been tried on a gigantic scale and proved to be not only a possible but the most desirable form of government yet attempted by mankind. What the future has to disclose it is idle to guess, but we may feel confident that the same wisdom and strength which has enabled our people to overcome their difficulties in the past will not fail them in conquering those to come, and long before another hundred years have rolled by we may rest assured that the American nation will be far ahead in the race for the leadership of the world.

TABLE OF THE PRESIDENTS.

NO.	PRESIDENT.	STATE.	BORN.	DIED.	TERM OF OFFICE.	BY WHOM ELECTED.	VICE-PRESIDENT.	SECRETARY OF STATE.
1	George Washington.	Virginia.	1732	1799	Two terms; 1789–1797.	Whole people.	John Adams.	Thomas Jefferson. Edmund Randolph. Timothy Pickering.
2	John Adams.	Massachusetts.	1735	1826	One term; 1797–1801.	Federalists	Thos. Jefferson.	Timothy Pickering. John Marshall.
3	Thomas Jefferson.	Virginia.	1743	1826	Two terms; 1801–1809.	Republicans	Aaron Burr. George Clinton.	James Madison.
4	James Madison.	Virginia.	1751	1836	Two terms; 1809–1817.	Republicans	George Clinton. Elbridge Gerry.	Robert Smith. James Monroe.
5	James Monroe.	Virginia.	1758	1831	Two terms; 1817–1825.	All parties.	Dan'l D. Tompkins	John Quincy Adams.
6	John Quincy Adams.	Massachusetts.	1767	1848	One term; 1825–1829.	House of Rep.	John C. Calhoun.	Henry Clay.
7	Andrew Jackson.	Tennessee.	1767	1845	Two terms; 1829–1837.	Democrats.	John C. Calhoun Mart. Van Buren	Martin Van Buren. Edward Livingston. Louis McLane.
8	Martin Van Buren.	New York.	1782	1862	One term; 1837–1841.	Democrats.	Rich'd M. Johnson.	John Forsyth.
9	William H. Harrison.	Ohio.	1773	1841	One month; 1841.	Whigs.	John Tyler.	Daniel Webster.
10	John Tyler.	Virginia.	1790	1862	3 yrs. and 11 months; 1841–1845	Whigs.		Hugh S. Legare. Abel P. Usher. John C. Calhoun.
11	James K. Polk.	Tennessee.	1795	1849	One term; 1845–1849.	Democrats.	George M. Dallas.	James Buchanan.
12	Zachary Taylor.	Louisiana.	1784	1850	1 year and 4 months; 1849–1850	Whigs.	Millard Fillmore.	John M. Clayton.
13	Millard Fillmore.	New York.	1800	1874	2 yrs. and 8 months; 1850–1853	Whigs.		Daniel Webster. Edward Everett.
14	Franklin Pierce.	N. Hampshire.	1804	1869	One term; 1853–1857.	Democrats.	William R. King.	William L. Marcy.
15	James Buchanan.	Pennsylvania	1791	1868	One term; 1857–1861.	Democrats.	J. C. Breckenridge.	Lewis Cass. Jeremiah S. Black.
16	Abraham Lincoln.	Illinois.	1809	1865	1 term and 1 month; 1861–1865	Republicans	Hannibal Hamlin Andrew Johnson.	Wm. H. Seward.
17	Andrew Johnson.	Tennessee.	1808	1875	3 yrs. and 11 months; 1865–1869	Republicans		William H. Seward.
18	Ulysses S. Grant.	Illinois.	1822	1885	Two terms; 1869–1877.	Republicans	Schuyler Colfax Henry Wilson	E. B. Washburne. Hamilton Fish.
19	Rutherford B. Hayes.	Ohio.	1822		One term; 1877–1881.	Republicans	Wm. A. Wheeler.	James G. Blaine.
20	James A. Garfield.	Ohio.	1831	1881	6 months and 15 days; 1881	Republicans	Chester A. Arthur.	James G. Blaine.
21	Chester A. Arthur.	New York.	1830	1886	3 yrs. and 5 months; 1881–1885.	Republicans		F. T. Frelinghuysen.
22	Grover Cleveland	New York.	1837		One term; 1885–1889.	Democrats	Thos. A. Hendricks.	Thomas F. Bayard.
23	Benjamin Harrison	Indiana	1833			Republicans	Levi P. Morton.	James G. Blaine.

TABLE OF ADMISSION OF STATES.

1	Delaware	accepted the Constitution			Dec. 7, 1787
2	Pennsylvania	"	"	"	Dec. 12, 1787
3	New Jersey	"	"	"	Dec. 18, 1787
4	Georgia	"	"	"	Jan. 2, 1788
5	Connecticut	"	"	"	Jan. 9, 1788
6	Massachusetts	"	"	"	Feb. 6, 1788
7	Maryland	"	"	"	Apr. 28, 1788
8	South Carolina	"	"	"	May 23, 1788
9	New Hampshire	"	"	"	June 21, 1788
10	Virginia	"	"	"	June 25, 1788
11	New York	"	"	"	July 26, 1788
12	North Carolina	"	"	"	Nov. 21, 1789
13	Rhode Island	"	"	"	May 29, 1790
14	Vermont	admitted to the Union			Mar. 4, 1791
15	Kentucky	"	"	"	June 1, 1792
16	Tennessee	"	"	"	June 1, 1796
17	Ohio	"	"	"	Nov. 29, 1802
18	Louisiana	"	"	"	Apr. 30, 1812
19	Indiana	"	"	"	Dec. 11, 1816
20	Mississippi	"	"	"	Dec. 10, 1817
21	Illinois	"	"	"	Dec. 3, 1818
22	Alabama	"	"	"	Dec. 14, 1819
23	Maine	"	"	"	Mar. 15, 1820
24	Missouri	"	"	"	Aug. 10, 1821
25	Arkansas	"	"	"	June 15, 1836
26	Michigan	"	"	"	Jan. 26, 1837
27	Florida	"	"	"	Mar. 3, 1845
28	Texas	"	"	"	Dec. 29, 1845
29	Iowa	"	"	"	Dec. 28, 1846
30	Wisconsin	"	"	"	May 29, 1848
31	California	"	"	"	Sept. 9, 1850
32	Minnesota	"	"	"	May 11, 1858
33	Oregon	"	"	"	Feb. 14, 1859
34	Kansas	"	"	"	Jan. 29, 1861
35	West Virginia	"	"	"	June 19, 1863
36	Nevada	"	"	"	Oct. 31, 1864
37	Nebraska	"	"	"	Mar. 1, 1867
38	Colorado	"	"	"	Aug. 1, 1876
39	North Dakota	"	"	"	Feb. 22, 1889
40	South Dakota	"	"	"	Feb. 22, 1889
41	Montana	"	"	"	Feb. 22, 1889
42	Washington	"	"	"	Feb. 22, 1889

CHRONOLOGICAL TABLE.

Discovery of America by Columbus	1492
Discovery of South America by Americus Vespucius	1497
Discovery of North America by the Cabots	1497
Discovery of the Gulf of St. Lawrence by the French	1504
Discovery of Florida by Ponce de Leon	1512
Discovery of the Pacific Ocean by Balboa	1513
Exploration of the Atlantic coast by Verrazzano	1524
Exploration of the St. Lawrence River by Cartier	1534
Attempt of the French to settle on the St. Lawrence	1540
Discovery of the Mississippi River by De Soto	1541
Attempt by the French to settle at Port Royal (S. C.)	1562
Attempt by the French to settle at Fort Carolina (Fla.)	1564
Settlement of St. Augustine (Fla.) by the Spanish	1565
Voyage of Frobisher	1576
Voyage of Drake	1579
Settlement of Santa Fé (N. M.) by the Spanish	1582
Attempt by Gilbert to settle in Newfoundland	1583
First attempt to settle on Roanoke Island (N. C.)	1585
Second attempt to settle on Roanoke Island (N. C.)	1587
Attempt to settle at Buzzard's Bay (Mass.)	1602
Settlement of Acadia (Nova Scotia) by the French	1605
Settlement of Jamestown (Va.)	1607
Settlement of Quebec by the French	1608
Discovery of the Hudson River	1609
Settlement of New York City by the Dutch	1614
Cultivation of tobacco begun in Virginia	1615
First American legislature met at Jamestown	1619
Introduction of slavery into America (Virginia)	1619
Settlement of New Plymouth (Mass.) by the Pilgrims	1620
Cultivation of cotton begun in Virginia	1621
Indian massacre at Jamestown	1622
Settlement of Dover and Portsmouth (N. H.)	1623
Virginia made a Royal Colony	1624
Settlement of Salem (Mass.) by the Puritans	1628
Settlement of Charlestown (Mass.) by the Puritans	1629
Settlement of Boston by the Puritans	1630
Settlement of St. Mary's (Md.) by the Roman Catholics	1634
Settlement of Saybrook, Windsor and Wethersfield (Conn.)	1635
Banishment of Roger Williams from Massachusetts	1635
Settlement of Hartford (Conn.)	1636
Settlement of Providence (R. I.)	1636
Founding of Harvard University	1636
Pequot War in Connecticut	1637
Settlement of Wilmington (Del.)	1638
Settlement of New Haven (Conn.)	1638
Indian disturbance in New York	1643
Grant of charter to Rhode Island	1644
Second Indian massacre in Virginia	1644
Boundary between New York and Connecticut arranged	1650
Passage of Navigation Act	1651
Conquest of Delaware by the Dutch of New York	1655
Persecution of the Quakers in Massachusetts	1656
Grant of charter to Connecticut	1662
Settlement of Elizabeth (N. J.)	1664
Conquest of New York by the English	1664
Settlement of North Carolina on the Chowan River	1664
Union of Connecticut and New Haven Colonies	1665
Settlement of Clarendon County (N. C.)	1665
Settlement of Newark (N. J.)	1666
Settlement of South Carolina on the Ashley River	1670
Holland's brief reconquest of New York	1673
King Philip's War in New England	1675
Bacon's Rebellion in Virginia	1676
Settlement of Burlington (N. J.)	1677
Settlement of Charleston (S. C.)	1680
Settlement of Pennsylvania begun by Penn	1682
Grant of Delaware to Penn by the Duke of York	1682
Settlement of Philadelphia	1683
Settlement of Annapolis (Md.)	1683
Andros appointed Governor of New England	1686
Union of Plymouth and Massachusetts Bay Colonies	1691
Founding of the College of William and Mary (Va.)	1692
Witchcraft delusion in Salem (Mass.)	1692
Founding of Yale University	1701
Settlement of Detroit (Mich.) by the French	1701
New Jersey made a Royal Colony	1702
Settlement of New Orleans (La.)	1718
Settlement of Baltimore (Md.)	1729
Separation of North and South Carolina	1729
Birth of George Washington Feb. 22,	1732
Settlement of Savannah (Ga.)	1733
Negro plot feared in New York	1740
Founding of the College of New Jersey	1746
Formation of the Ohio Company	1749
Founding of the University of Pennsylvania	1749
Georgia made a Royal Colony	1752
Founding of Columbia College	1754
Outbreak of the French and Indian War	1754
Capture of Fort Necessity by the French	1754
Defeat of Braddock by the French	1755
Capture of Louisberg from the French	1758
Capture of Fort Du Quesne from the French	1758
Defeat of the English and Americans at Ticonderoga	1758
Capture of Fort Frontenac from the French	1758
Surrender of Quebec by the French	1759
Surrender of Montreal by the French	1760

HISTORY OF THE UNITED STATES.

End of French and Indian War.................. 1763
Cession of Canada to Great Britain.............. 1763
Boundary between Pennsylvania and Maryland
  (" Mason and Dixon's line ") arranged.......... 1763
Passage of the Stamp Act....................... 1765
Repeal of the Stamp Act........................ 1766
Passage of the new tax bill.................... 1767
Arrival of British troops at Boston............ 1768
Repeal of duties excepting on tea.............. 1770
Destruction of tea in Boston harbor............ 1773
Closing of the Port of Boston by Parliament.... 1774
Meeting of the Continental Congress at Philadelphia. 1774
Battle of Lexington.....................April 19, 1775
Capture of Ticonderoga by the Americans. May 10, 1775
Capture of Crown Point by the Americans. May 12, 1775
Washington appointed Commander-in-chief. June 15, 1775
Battle of Bunker Hill....................June 17, 1775
Capture of Montreal by the Americans....Nov. 13, 1775
Repulse of the Americans at Quebec.....Dec. 31, 1775
Evacuation of Boston by the British.....March 17, 1776
Declaration of Independence.............July 4, 1776
Battle of Long Island...................Aug. 27, 1776
Evacuation of New York by the Americans. Sept. 14, 1776
Battle of Trenton......................Dec. 25, 1776
Battle of Princeton....................Jan. 3, 1777
Capture of Ticonderoga by the British..July 5, 1777
Battle of Bennington...................Aug. 16, 1777
Battle of Brandywine...................Sept. 11, 1777
Battle of Bemis Heights................Sept. 19, 1777
Capture of Philadelphia by the British.. Sept. 26, 1777
Battle of Germantown....................Oct. 4, 1777
Battle of Stillwater....................Oct. 7, 1777
Surrender of Burgoyne at Saratoga........Oct. 17, 1777
Treaty with France ....Feb. 6, 1778
Evacuation of Philadelphia by the British.. June 18, 1778
Battle of Monmouth.....................June 28, 1778
Capture of Savannah by the British......Dec. 29, 1778
Naval victory of Paul Jones............Sept. 23, 1779
Repulse of Americans at Savannah.......Sept. 23, 1779
Capture of Charleston (S. C.) by the British,
                                       May 12, 1780
Battle of Camden (N. C.)................Aug. 16, 1780
Treason of Benedict Arnold..............Sept., 1780
Execution of Major André................Oct. 2, 1780
Adoption of the Articles of Confederation. March 1, 1781
Surrender of Cornwallis at Yorktown......Oct. 19, 1781
Treaty of peace with Great Britain......Sept. 3, 1783
Evacuation of New York by the British...Nov. 25, 1783
Meeting of the Constitutional Convention at Philadelphia.......................... May 25, 1787
Adoption of the Ordinance of 1787........July 13, 1787
Adoption of the Constitution by the Convention............................Sept. 17, 1787
Adoption of the Constitution by the ninth State,
                                       June 21, 1788
Meeting of the first Congress at New York. March 4, 1789
Inauguration of President Washington....April 30, 1789

Adoption of the first ten Amendments to the Constitution,.................................... 1791
Admission of the State of Vermont........Feb. 18, 1791
Admission of the State of Kentucky.......June 1, 1792
Invention of the cotton-gin by Whitney.......... 1793
Admission of the State of Tennessee......June 1, 1796
Inauguration of President John Adams...March 4, 1797
Adoption of the eleventh Amendment to the Constitution 1798
War with France threatened,............... 1798
Passage of the Alien and Sedition Laws......June, 1798
Capture of " L'Insurgente," by the " Constellation" ....Feb. 10, 1799
Death of Washington....................Dec. 14, 1799
Removal of the national capital to Washington,
                                       June 15, 1800
Inauguration of President Jefferson......March 4, 1801
Declaration of War by Tripoli............May 14, 1801
Admission of the State of Ohio ....Nov. 29, 1802
Purchase of Louisiana from France ......April 30, 1803
Adoption of the twelfth Amendment to the Constitution 1804
Expedition of Lewis and Clarke through the Oregon
  country..................................... 1804
Destruction of the " Philadelphia " by Lieut. Decatur......................................Feb. 3, 1804
Duel between Hamilton and Burr.........July 11, 1804
Treaty of peace with Tripoli................June, 1805
Blockade of France proclaimed by England...May, 1806
Blockade of Great Britain proclaimed by France,
                                       Nov., 1806
Burr accused of treason........................ 1807
Invention of the steamboat by Fulton.......... 1807
British Orders in Council forbidding trade with
  France...............................Nov. 11, 1807
Napoleon's Milan Decree forbidding trade with
  Great Britain........................Dec. 17, 1807
Passage of the Embargo Act ....Dec. 22, 1807
Importation of slaves forbidden.................. 1808
Passage of the Non-Intercourse Act......March 1, 1809
Inauguration of President Madison ......March 4, 1809
Battle of Tippecanoe.......................Nov. 7, 1811
Admission of the State of Louisiana......April 30, 1812
Declaration of war against Great Britain.. June 18, 1812
The "Essex" captures the " Alert " ......Aug. 13, 1812
Surrender of Detroit by Hull to the British. Aug. 16, 1812
The " Constitution" captures the " Guerriere,"
                                       Aug. 19, 1812
The "Wasp" captures the "Frolic "......Oct. 18, 1812
The "Wasp" captured by the "Poictiers"..Oct. 18, 1812
The " United States" captures the "Macedonian,"
                                       Oct. 25, 1812
The "Constitution" captures the "Java"..Dec. 29, 1812
Massacre at the Raisin River...............Jan. 22, 1813
The " Hornet " captures the " Peacock "..Feb. 24, 1813
The " Chesapeake " captured by the " Shannon,"
                                       June 1, 1813

CHRONOLOGICAL TABLE.   151

Massacre at Fort Mims .... Aug. 30, 1813	Death of President Harrison .... April 6, 1841
Perry's victory on Lake Erie .... Sept. 10, 1813	Inauguration of President Tyler .... April 6, 1841
Battle of the Thames .... Oct. 5, 1813	Boundary and extradition treaty with Great Britain, 1842
Battle of Tohopeka .... March 27, 1814	End of the war with the Seminole Indians 1842
The "Essex" captured by the "Phœbe" and the "Cherub" .... March 28, 1814	Invention of the electric telegraph by Morse 1845
	Annexation of Texas .... March 1, 1845
The "Peacock" captures the "Epervier".. April 29, 1814	Admission of the State of Florida .... March 3, 1845
The "Wasp" captures the "Reindeer" ... June 28, 1814	Inauguration of President Polk .... March 4, 1845
Battle of Lundy's Lane .... July 25, 1814	Admission of the State of Texas .... Dec. 29, 1845
Burning of the City of Washington .... Aug. 24, 1814	Invention of the sewing-machine by Elias Howe ... 1846
The "Wasp" captures the "Avon" .... Sept. 1, 1814	Northwestern boundary decided 1846
Macdonough's victory on Lake Champlain. Sept. 11, 1814	Passage of low tariff act 1846
Hartford Convention .... Dec. 15, 1814	First use of ether in surgery 1846
Treaty of peace with Great Britain .... Dec. 24, 1814	Declaration of war against Mexico .... May 13, 1846
Battle of New Orleans .... Jan. 8, 1815	Capture of Monterey .... Sept. 24, 1846
The "President" captured by a British fleet. Jan. 15, 1815	Admission of the State of Iowa .... Dec. 28, 1846
The "Constitution" captures the "Cyane" and the "Levant" .... Feb. 20, 1815	Battle of Buena Vista .... Feb. 24, 1847
	Capture of Vera Cruz .... March 27, 1847
The "Hornet" captures the "Penguin". March 23, 1815	Battle of Cerro Gordo .... April 18, 1847
The "Peacock" captures the "Nautilus". June 30, 1815	Capture of Chapultepec .... Sept. 13, 1847
Admission of the State of Indiana .... Dec. 11, 1816	Capture of the City of Mexico .... Sept. 14, 1847
Inauguration of President Monroe .... March 4, 1817	Discovery of gold in California .... Jan. 19, 1848
Admission of the State of Mississippi ..... Dec. 10, 1817	Treaty of peace with Mexico .... Feb. 2, 1848
Admission of the State of Illinois .... Dec. 3, 1818	Admission of the State of Wisconsin ..... May 29, 1848
Admission of the State of Alabama ..... Dec. 14, 1819	Inauguration of President Taylor .... March 5, 1849
Passage of the Missouri Compromise Act. March 3, 1820	Death of President Taylor .... July 9, 1850
Admission of the State of Maine .... March 15, 1820	Inauguration of President Fillmore .... July 10, 1850
Purchase of Florida from Spain .... July 1, 1821	Passage of fugitive slave law .... Sept., 1850
Admission of the State of Missouri .... Aug. 10, 1821	Admission of the State of California ...... Sept. 9, 1850
First use in America of illuminating gas 1822	Inauguration of President Pierce .... March 4, 1853
Promulgation of the Monroe Doctrine 1823	Repeal of the Missouri Compromise .... May, 1854
Visit of Lafayette to the United States 1824	Financial panic 1857
Adoption of a protective tariff 1824	Dred Scott decision 1857
Inauguration of President John Q. Adams.. March 4, 1825	Inauguration of President Buchanan ..... March 4, 1857
Completion of the Erie Canal .... Oct., 1825	Discovery of silver in Nevada 1858
Death of John Adams and Thomas Jefferson.. July 4, 1826	Admission of the State of Minnesota ..... May 11, 1858
First railroads built in America 1827	Admission of the State of Oregon .... Feb. 14, 1859
Adoption of a higher protective tariff 1828	Discovery of petroleum in Pennsylvania ...... Aug., 1859
Inauguration of President Jackson .... March 4, 1829	Raid of John Brown .... Oct., 1859
Sect of Mormons founded 1830	Secession of South Carolina .... Dec. 20, 1860
Beginning of the spoils system 1830	Secession of ten other States 1861
Black Hawk War 1832	Admission of the State of Kansas .... Jan. 29, 1861
Adoption of new protective tariff 1832	Organization of the Confederacy .... Feb. 4, 1861
Attempt at nullification by South Carolina 1832	Inauguration of President Lincoln .... March 4, 1861
Adoption of a compromise tariff 1833	Evacuation of Fort Sumter .... April 13, 1861
Removal of government money from U. S. Bank.. 1833	First bloodshed of the Civil War at Baltimore, April 19, 1861
Disagreement with France 1834	
Invention of the reaping machine 1834	Richmond made the Confederate capital. . July 20, 1861
Invention of the revolver 1835	Battle of Bull Run .... July 21, 1861
Beginning of the war with the Seminole Indians ... 1835	Capture of Roanoke Island .... Feb. 8, 1862
Great fire in New York City 1835	Battle between the "Monitor" and the "Merrimac," March 9, 1862
National debt paid off 1835	
Admission of the State of Arkansas .... June 15, 1836	Battle of Shiloh .... April 6, 1862
Financial panic 1837	Capture of New Orleans .... April 25, 1862
Admission of the State of Michigan .... Jan. 26, 1837	Capture of Corinth .... May 30, 1862
Inauguration of President Van Buren .... March 4, 1837	Bragg's invasion of Tennessee and Kentucky. Sept., 1862
Inauguration of President W. H. Harrison. March 4, 1841	Battle of Antietam .... Sept. 17, 1862

HISTORY OF THE UNITED STATES.

Battle of Fredericksburg.................. Dec. 13, 1862
Emancipation Proclamation................ Jan. 1, 1863
Battle of Chancellorsville.................. May 2, 1863
Admission of the State of West Virginia.. June 20, 1863
Seizure of Mexico by the French .... July, 1863
Battle of Gettysburg...................... July 3, 1863
Capture of Vicksburg...................... July 4, 1863
Battle of Chickamauga.................. Sept. 19, 1863
Battles of Lookout Mountain and Missionary Ridge,
  Nov. 24, 1863
Battles of the Wilderness.................... May, 1864
Battles at Spottsylvania Court-House....... May, 1864
Battle of Cold Harbor.................... June 3, 1864
Battle between the "Kearsarge" and the "Alabama"................................ June 19, 1864
Capture of Atlanta....................... Sept. 2, 1864
Battle of Winchester................... Sept. 19, 1864
Battle of Cedar Creek................... Oct. 19, 1864
Admission of the State of Nevada........ Oct. 31, 1864
Battle of Nashville..................... Dec. 15, 1864
Capture of Savannah.................... Dec. 21, 1864
Capture of Fort Fisher................... Jan. 15, 1865
Capture of Charleston................... Feb. 18, 1865
Battle of Goldsboro................... March 19, 1865
Capture of Petersburg................... April 2, 1865
Capture of Richmond.................... April 3, 1865
Surrender of Lee....................... April 9, 1865
Assassination of Lincoln............... April 14, 1865
Inauguration of President Johnson....... April 15, 1865
Surrender of Johnston................. April 26, 1865
Capture of Jefferson Davis.............. May 11, 1865
Adoption of the thirteenth Amendment to the Constitution................................. Dec., 1865
Telegraphic cable laid between Europe and America..................................... July, 1866
Passage of Reconstruction Acts........... March, 1867
Evacuation of Mexico by the French ...... March, 1867
Passage of Tenure-of-Office Act.......... March, 1867
Admission of the State of Nebraska...... March 1, 1867
Declaration of amnesty by the President... Sept. 8, 1867
Purchase of Alaska from Russia .... Oct. 9, 1867

Impeachment of President Johnson....... Jan. 24, 1868
Adoption of the fourteenth Amendment to the Constitution............................... July, 1868
Inauguration of President Grant......... March 4, 1869
Completion of the Central Pacific Railroad. May 10, 1869
Adoption of the fifteenth Amendment to the Constitution................................ March, 1870
Treaty of Washington (with Great Britain) . May 8, 1871
Great fire in Chicago..................... Oct. 7, 1871
Award of "Alabama" damages by Geneva tribunal,
  Sept. 14, 1872
Great fire in Boston..................... Nov. 9, 1872
Financial panic............................. 1873
Demonetization of silver...................... 1873
Opening of Centennial Exposition at Philadelphia,
  May 10, 1876
Admission of the State of Colorado........ Aug. 1, 1876
Meeting of the Presidential Electoral Commission,
  Feb., 1877
Invention of the telephone by Bell............ 1877
Inauguration of President Hayes........ March 4, 1877
Railroad riots............................. July, 1877
First use of the electric light.................. 1878
Remonetization of silver...................... 1878
Resumption of specie payments.......... Jan. 1, 1879
Inauguration of President Garfield ...... March 4, 1881
Shooting of President Garfield .... July 2, 1881
Death of President Garfield............. Sept. 19, 1881
Inauguration of President Arthur .... Sept. 20, 1881
Passage of anti-polygamy law................. 1882
Passage of civil service reform law............. 1883
Inauguration of President Cleveland...... March 4, 1885
Rank of General restored to Grant........ March, 1885
Death of Grant........................ July 23, 1885
Fisheries dispute with Canada................. 1888
Tariff agitation............................. 1888
Passage of Act for admission of States of North Dakota, South Dakota, Washington and Montana................................ Feb. 22, 1889
Inaguration of President Benjamin Harrison,
  March 4, 1889

www.ingramcontent.com/pod-product-compliance
Lightning Source LLC
Chambersburg PA
CBHW030306170426
43202CB00009B/895